A Practical Guide to

Financial Management

for Charities and Voluntary Organisations

Kate Sayer

DIRECTORY OF SOCIAL CHANGE

Published by
The Directory of Social Change
24 Stephenson Way
London NW1 2DP
Tel: 08740 77 77 07, fax: 020 7391 4808
email: publications@dsc.org.uk
from whom further copies and a full publications list are available.
In association with Sayer Vincent
8 Angel Gate, City Road, London EC1V 2SJ Tel: 020 7841 6360
e-mail:info@sayervincent.co.uk

The Directory of Social Change is Registered Charity no. 800517

First edition published 1998
Second edition published 2002
Third edition published 2007

ISBN-13 978 1 903991 72 5

British Library Cataloguing in Publication Data
A catalogue record for this book is available from the British Library

Cover design by Kate Bass
Designed and typeset by Keystroke
Printed and bound by Antony Rowe

Directory of Social Change London Office:
08450 77 77 07

Directory of Social Change Liverpool Office:
Federation House, Hope Street, Liverpool L1 9BW
0151 708 0136

Contents

Foreword

Understanding financial issues is a key skill for everyone who works within a charity. In fact, the greater the depth of knowledge throughout the organisation the greater the financial control, and, more importantly, the better the charity will be able to maximise the quality of its services to its beneficiaries. Delivery starts with a strong and achievable strategy that relates well to the charity's mission, and it is with this idea that the book opens. The early chapters go on to cover financial management of a charity in a straightforward and pragmatic way, using clear and well-explained examples.

The book flows easily into chapters on preparing, presenting and interpreting charity accounts. In recent years there has been an improvement in the quality of charity accounts as a result of both the developments in the charity SORP and the recognition by many that accounts are not only a regulatory requirement but also an excellent opportunity to market the charity to its various existing and potential stakeholders. Good trustees' annual reports and accounts should show the impact that the charity is making and where it is on its strategic journey. For this purpose the charity must get the accounting basics right. Kate takes us through these areas step by step, using helpful case studies.

The final chapters of the book cover the taxation of charities; these are complex and difficult areas even for the most experienced of financial professionals in the charity sector, yet here the basics are laid out clearly and are easy to follow.

At its best accounting is simple. Unfortunately, at times it is made difficult through bad application of the basics. Good financial information should be presented in a way that the user has what he or she needs to make well-informed decisions to improve the charity's performance. This book does just that, providing a clear-cut guide to financial management and accounting. Readers who are new to charity finance will easily grasp the theory, techniques and skills required, and those who are experienced financial professionals will have a good reference guide to hand.

Keith Hickey
Chief Executive, Charity Finance Directors' Group

Introduction

Financial management is about good stewardship of the assets available to a charity, as well as ensuring that the organisation has the resources it needs to fulfil its objects and plans. The legal responsibility for the good financial management of a charity ultimately rests with the trustees; although in larger charities paid staff will have a significant role to play.

Financial management is part of management as a whole and should not be seen as a separate activity left entirely to accountants or the finance department. This book is addressed largely to those without an accounting background and aims to equip them with the basic knowledge and skills they need to exercise good financial management practices. It is only a starting point, however, and managers will need to enhance their skills and develop good financial management practice through experience.

Although written for charities, the book will also be relevant to voluntary and other non-profit-making organisations that are not registered charities. The principles of good financial management apply to all these organisations and most will have a management structure similar to charities.

The first few chapters cover the basics of financial planning, including tasks such as costing, drawing up a budget, monitoring cashflow, managing risk, and presenting and using financial information to make decisions. The second section covers the actual production and interpretation of accounts, including basic bookkeeping, preparing annual accounts, the Charity Commission's Statement of Recommended Practice (SORP), and annual auditing requirements. These sections have been updated in the third edition for the revised charity SORP issued in March 2005.

The financial management of charities must be understood against the appropriate legal background. Charities are affected by many different laws in addition to charity law, and some reference is made to these as appropriate. Tax laws affect charities in specific ways, and so chapters have been devoted to trading and VAT in the final section of the book. The third edition has been updated to reflect the law up to May 2007, with some references to the Charities Act 2006 and the Companies Act 2006 where these affecting accounting and auditing.

This book does not aim to be comprehensive and so the Further Reading section at the end lists other books which cover relevant and related areas – such as employment law – in more depth. In addition, regular updated information is available on the Sayer Vincent website www.sayervincent.co.uk

Kate Sayer is a chartered accountant with over 20 years experience of the charity and not-for-profit sector. She is a partner with Sayer Vincent, a specialist consultancy focussing on IT, audit, governance and financial management issues for charities and not-for-profit organisations.

Sayer Vincent
8 Angel Gate
City Road
London
EC1V 2SJ

020 7841 6360

svinfo@sayervincent.co.uk
www.sayervincent.co.uk

1 Financial planning

THE PLANNING CYCLE

Financial planning does not start with numbers. In fact, it is impossible to start a financial forecast without some idea of what you want to do and how. Good budgets can only be produced as a result of good underlying plans. Since there are always a number of variable factors, there may be considerable changes over the life of a plan. It is appropriate to think of the whole process as a cycle, because you have to review plans and budgets all the time.

The planning cycle

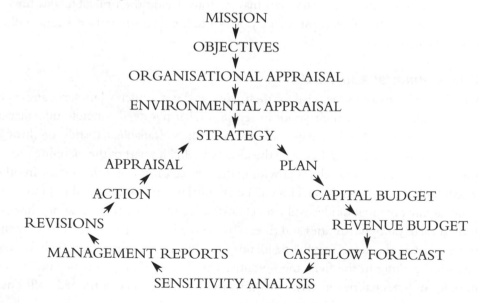

MISSION
↓
OBJECTIVES
↓
ORGANISATIONAL APPRAISAL
↓
ENVIRONMENTAL APPRAISAL
↓
STRATEGY

APPRAISAL   PLAN

ACTION   CAPITAL BUDGET

REVISIONS   REVENUE BUDGET

MANAGEMENT REPORTS   CASHFLOW FORECAST

SENSITIVITY ANALYSIS

Mission

Most organisations now have a mission statement. In fact, charities and voluntary organisations have always been fairly clear about their objectives, as these have to be established in order to set up the charity. Charities are motivated by the cause and this is usually well known to staff, volunteers and trustees. On the other hand, the process of drawing up a mission statement that focuses everyone's attention on the real purposes of the organisation can be beneficial.

Objectives

Whilst the overall mission of the charity may be obvious, the objectives for the medium term will need careful thought. Objectives will often be the building bricks that help the organisation achieve its mission. For example, one objective might be the creation of a national service from a current base of one or two offices. Or a charity might decide that its objective should be to offer a place on a training course to every young person in its area of operation. At this stage of the planning process the objectives may be stated in fairly general terms, but should give focus to the organisation's work. The organisation may also decide on some specifically financial objectives, such as achieving a certain level of general reserves.

Organisational appraisal

Having decided on its general direction for the next few years, the organisation then needs to look at itself and assess its strengths and weaknesses in relation to the objectives it has set. This process may identify new skills and/or additional resources that will be needed – which could be staff, new premises or updated computer equipment. Identifying strengths and weaknesses may help to decide the timetable and how to progress towards the objectives; you may decide to build on strengths first, and address the weaknesses later.

Environmental appraisal

Charities need to assess the need for their work, just as commercial undertakings need to assess the market for their goods or services. Charities need concrete information about the 'market', which may come from publicly available statistics, or through research or information gathered by the charity itself. This part of the planning process should also consider who else is providing the service or meeting the need – in other words look at the competition. This will be essential when putting together fundraising plans, as any potential funder will expect answers to such questions. The organisation should focus on opportunities and threats presented by external forces. The outcome of this part of the work may be to identify some constraining factors, such as other charities working in the field, the potential withdrawal of government funding, the number of potential beneficiaries or difficulty recruiting suitably trained staff. These factors will all need to be fed into the plans.

Strategy

The strategy tries to set out the overall approach or plan for getting the organisation from A to B, where A is where it is now and B is where it wants to be in so many years' time, as expressed in the objectives. So, for example, if one of the objectives is to ensure that all beneficiaries can access the charity's services anywhere in the country, then the strategy needs to set out the actions needed to achieve the desired outcome.

Plan

The plan will go into more detail than the strategy and may be sub-divided, for example into a fundraising plan, an IT plan, a staffing plan, and so on. The financial plan is just one of the plans. While the objectives and strategy should be established at the beginning of the planning cycle and remain more or less the same for a long period, the plans will need to be reviewed and refined as progress is made. For example, the strategy may remain the same, but the timescale in which it can be achieved may have to be reviewed again and again. Plans are the short-term action plans of the organisation, looking about one year ahead.

Capital budget

This will usually set out the costings for larger projects, but can also be used for smaller amounts of one-off expenditure. A capital budget needs to look about five years ahead, although changes may be needed as you go forward. It is more usual for the timing, rather than the overall budget, to change. The capital budget will dovetail in with other plans, for example the IT plan should lead to a plan for acquisition of computers and other equipment. Notes to explain the figures in the budget are essential. You should make a note of implications for revenue budgets and cashflow (see below) for incorporation into those forecasts. For example, the maintenance for new equipment should be included in the revenue budget.

Revenue budget

The revenue budget has to be built up from the detailed plans for staffing, fundraising, IT and other operational areas. Clearly, one of the purposes of the revenue budget is to see how the pieces of the jigsaw fit together. Incoming resources have to match the spending plans; the spending plans have to be the best use of resources. Revenue budgets should be prepared in detail for the year ahead, and in outline for several years beyond. They may have to be changed many times, but it is important that the organisation has some feel for the financial implications of its objectives and plans. Assumptions will have to be made in preparing the revenue budgets: these should be written down and kept for future reference.

Cashflow forecast

The cashflow forecast will be based on the detailed plans, the revenue budget and the capital budget. It will show whether the organisation will have the cash resources to meet the timetable of the plan. If the plan requires expansion and spending before acquiring additional incoming resources, this will be a strain on cash resources. The cashflow forecast will identify the organisation's working capital.

Sensitivity analysis

This technique needs to be applied to the most uncertain elements in your budgets and forecasts. You should calculate the effects of changes to test your financial plans for robustness. Ask yourself, for example, 'what if staff pay goes up by seven per cent instead of four per cent?' Can the organisation pass on the increase to purchasers of its services? Can it absorb the extra cost? Can costs be cut elsewhere? This exercise may enable the organisation to prepare a certain number of contingency plans or different options it can switch to depending on events.

Management reports

Reports for management should be comparisons between actual financial results and the agreed budgets, so that performance can be monitored. The notes on assumptions will be needed, in order to ascertain which element(s) of the plan did not happen as expected.

Revisions

Revisions follow on naturally from the reporting, as learning is part of the cycle. Plans improve as the organisation gets better at reading the information available.

Action

An important part of the planning cycle for a voluntary organisation is the trustees' approval of the plans. This gives staff a mandate to get on with the work in the plan and implicit approval to spend funds in accordance with the plans and budgets. Clearly, authorisation may still be needed for certain actions, but clear, agreed plans and budgets will help the organisation to take action.

Appraisal

This means an appraisal for the whole organisation, not just individual plans. You also need to assess the planning process – how well did it work? Does the budgeting process work for both trustees and staff? Appraisal also means that you have to set performance indicators at the beginning of the planning cycle – how will we measure the success of a plan? This is about qualitative as well as financial measures.

In summary, the whole planning process is a cycle, because you do not ever stop planning. Plans should not be drawn up and then put on a shelf. In order to implement them, plans have to be a live part of what the organisation is doing. You do not need to rewrite them every five minutes: the written version is only one part of the process. The activity of planning and having a planning framework is important for an organisation to be responsive and be able to cope with change. Such organisations are usually more successful at their fundraising, as the planning framework is apparent in all their dealings with potential funders. It does take some time to develop a planning process that involves people and works for your organisation. That should not put you off. You do not have to be perfect at planning before you can start. The most important thing is to start. *Then* you can improve!

The rest of this chapter will look at practical ways in which you can draw together elements of a plan, concentrating on the financial aspects. Different elements will have greater or lesser importance for different organisations, but the formats and techniques described below should give you some templates you can use as appropriate for your situation.

COSTING

In order to budget properly you need to understand how costs arise and what affects them. Figures in budgets or accounts are meaningless unless they can be put into a context. You will not draw up a good revenue budget for next year by taking last year's accounts or budget and adding five per cent to everything.

Example

In last year's accounts the amount for staff costs for the year was £154,896, including employer's national insurance. You estimate that the pay rise will be five per cent and so want to put £162,641 into the revenue budget, showing a five per cent increase on the accounts figure. This will be inaccurate, because included in the accounts figure are the effects of:

■ one staff member leaving half way through the year, and the replacement starting one month before the year end

■ one staff member being on maternity leave for three months, with no cover through the staff costs budget. Agency staff have been used, but this comes under a different budget heading, for relief staff.

You also know that one member of staff will be retiring half way through the coming year and there are no plans to replace them. Drawing up a more detailed plan, showing staff who will be in post for the coming year, you also realise that some staff are due increments and others are already at the top of their scale. In addition, the pay increase comes half way through the year. A more detailed calculation reveals that the budget ought to be £155,000 – about the same as last year's expenditure.

Staff costs are frequently a major proportion of a voluntary organisation's expenditure and so it pays to spend some time to build up that item. You will also find out how your organisation treats expenditure such as temporary cover. Other expenditure items will not necessarily involve so much effort. For example, you have a photocopier lease and repayments are fixed over the term of the lease. So there is no need to add five per cent to last year's accounting figure for the next year's budget. The approach 'add x per cent onto all expenditure headings' will produce inaccurate budgets, which means that they will probably be ignored, rather than used as a management tool. Even if you are a grant-funded group and you know that your funding is going to increase (or decrease) by a fixed percentage, you cannot prepare a useful expenditure budget by simply marking up existing headings by a fixed percentage.

So it is a good idea to understand more about the costs in the organisation. By looking at historic information and investigating the basis of the amounts shown in financial accounts, you will learn about the types of costs, what makes them increase or decrease and how predictable they are.

Reviewing the past – checklist

The following questions may assist in gathering relevant information, but extend the list as necessary:

1. How many members did the organisation have last year? How many sites did we cover? What services did we provide and to what extent?

2. How many staff did we employ? Check on part-time or staff only employed for part of the year. What posts did they fill and were there vacancies during the year?

3. What salary scales apply?

4. How did we account for temporary or relief staff?

5. How many volunteers did we have and what work did they do?

6. Were there any one-off expenses that will not apply again (e.g. cost of moving to new premises)?

7. How much do our premises cost us to run? Are there any factors that will change that (e.g. rent reviews)?

8. Which costs related specifically to certain projects (e.g. cost of printing a report relating to a funded project)?

9. Are there any time-limited projects? Are their costs separately identified?

10. Are there any particular policy decisions that affect our expenditure (e.g. training policy, policy for charging fees)?

11. What is the state of our equipment (fixed assets) – might it need replacing – and how has it been funded in the past?

12. Do we have ongoing commitments (e.g. photocopier lease)?

New organisations

If you are setting up a new organisation, think about the activities you will be undertaking and start a list of cost headings, without making any attempt at this stage to put figures beside them. You can undertake the research later to get estimates of the costs.

Analysing costs

Variable and fixed costs

Once you have done some investigation into the cost headings of your organisation, you should be able to split costs into variable and fixed costs.

■ Variable costs vary in proportion to the level of activity of the organisation.

■ Fixed costs are usually the overheads of an organisation or department and will be incurred regardless of the level of activity. It does not mean that the actual amount in the budget is fixed; it means that the *volume* needed does not vary greatly, even though the *price* may vary. So, for example, you would need the same amount of heating in a building regardless of the number of projects being run from it.

Direct and indirect costs

Classifying costs as direct or indirect is another way of looking at them in relation to the structure of the organisation and the 'department' in which the cost arises. Larger charities tend to have departmental structures: there will be a number of charitable projects, often self-financing, and a central administration department, which usually has little income of its own.

■ Direct costs can be identified as the costs directly attributable to a particular project or department.

■ Indirect costs relate to the organisation as a whole. Central administration costs are indirect costs to the organisation, since they cover all projects but generally do not relate specifically to any one.

Understanding costs

Both these methods of analysing costs can be relevant at the same time. Variable costs are often, but not always, also direct costs. Variable or fixed is a question of how the costs behave in relation to the level of activity; direct or indirect is a question of where the cost arises.

Looking at your list of cost headings, can you analyse them into the different types of costs?

- Is it a cost the organisation incurs regardless of activities or funding? For example lease commitments, rent and insurance on premises (*fixed costs*)?

- Is it a cost only arising because you plan to undertake a certain activity? For example hall hire for an event (*direct cost*)?

- Is it a cost that increases when you expand the organisation? For example staff travel, staff training (*direct cost* – dependent on the number of staff)?

- Is it a cost that varies to some extent, but has a core cost which is unavoidable? For example telephone – the rental costs and a few calls are inevitable, but extra activity pushes up the calls costs (*mixed cost*).

Understanding your costs will help you to make more accurate forecasts, and also to interpret management accounts and reports. Fixed costs are generally unavoidable costs, in the short term at least. It is usually easiest to group these together (for example all premises costs) and the budget estimates can probably be prepared without a great deal of effort. Because these costs are unavoidable, staff and trustees should not spend a great deal of time discussing them. The notes to the budget should explain the basis for the estimates in the budget and so any major mistakes should be picked up.

Contribution analysis

Once you have identified the cost headings that are likely to be your fixed costs, you should be able to use this information to draw a picture of the organisation's overall cost structure. The total of the organisation's fixed costs is the amount of *contribution* needed from income-earning projects, grants and other activities in order for the organisation to break even. These activities also have to cover their variable costs, so this is not the same as the total income needed for a particular project.

Example

The Borchester Community Centre has three projects and operates from small premises. It employs a permanent centre co-ordinator, and project staff are hired on a sessional basis. It has prepared the following information about costs:

- Centre co-ordinator's salary and national insurance £16,000

- Premises' fixed costs amount to approximately £15,000

- Project A needs sessional staff costing £3,000 and materials costing £800

- Project B needs sessional staff costing £5,000, additional telephone costs estimated at £900 and extra print and stationery costs of £1,000

- Project C needs sessional staff costing £4,000 and additional travel costs of £500

This information can be more usefully presented:

	Project A	Project B	Project C	TOTAL
Project costs				
Sessional staff	3,000	5,000	4,000	12,000
Materials	800	800		
Additional telephone	900	900		
Extra print and stationery	1,000	1,000		
Additional travel			500	500
Total direct costs of projects	3,800	6,900	4,500	15,200
Centre fixed costs				
Centre co-ordinator's salary and NI				16,000
Premises' fixed costs				15,000
Contribution needed from projects				31,000
TOTAL INCOME NEEDED				46,200

The Borchester Community Centre needs a total income of £46,200, but £31,000 of this relates to fixed costs and only £15,200 to projects. Each project needs to have sufficient income to cover its own direct costs and make a contribution towards the fixed costs of the organisation. Alternatively, a core grant is needed to cover the fixed costs.

This example draws out two points:

■ You need to obtain funding for projects that covers the direct costs of the project and also makes a contribution to the fixed costs of the organisation.

■ The fixed costs will seem high in relation to projects unless you have enough projects. There will be a certain minimum of fixed costs (also known as core costs) for all organisations. You need to find the right balance between projects and core costs.

An individual project's contribution is calculated by looking at its income and deducting the direct costs.

Using contribution analysis for decision-making

The approach in the above example can be helpful, as it also highlights the cost saving if the organisation decides to close down one of the projects. None of the central fixed costs would be reduced and the only saving would be the direct project costs.

In a similar way, it is unlikely that the fixed costs would change if the organisation started one more project. So the financial decision about taking on a new project hinges on the *contribution* the project will be able to make. In other words, does it bring sufficient income to cover its own direct costs plus some more? There would be a limit on the number of projects that could be run from the existing premises or co-ordinated by one member of staff, but until that limit is reached, the money spent on overheads is not providing the maximum financial benefit.

Once maximum capacity has been reached, the next project the organisation considers needs to be looked at carefully. In financial terms, the cost of taking on that project is not only its direct costs, but also the whole of the increase in fixed costs associated with the necessary increase in capacity. Because that project is, for example, forcing a move to new premises and/or additional core staffing, it must show that it can bring in enough income to make a sufficient contribution to these extra costs.

This may seem illogical in some ways. It could be argued that one project will not be able to carry a big increase in fixed costs, and fixed costs should be spread fairly across all projects. The answer is that both views are correct. For the purposes of decision-making, you should look at the impact the new activity will have on the organisation. If the new project or activity will force up fixed costs, then those costs are associated with that decision. In financial terms, the new activity should only be taken on if it can cover all the costs associated with the decision.

Break-even analysis for decision-making

Break-even analysis is an extension of the process of identifying the contribution a project or activity makes. For the organisation as a whole to break even, the contribution from all activities must be equal to fixed costs. This is also true of smaller-scale activities, such as fundraising events, where it can be useful to identify the fixed costs and the break-even point. Fundraising events can be high-risk and this can be identified in financial terms by the probability of the event breaking even.

Example

A charitable trust wants to hold a fundraising concert. The event will be held at a concert hall, which has a capacity of 5,000. There will also be a reception afterwards where wine will be served. The organisers plan to sell tickets at £10 and glasses of wine for £1. The concert hall will cost £1,000 to hire, publicity leaflets will cost £400 to print and wine will cost 50p per glass (sale or return basis). It will employ 10 waiters for the evening, who will be paid £50 each.

The fixed costs of this event:

Hall hire	1,000
Publicity leaflets	400
Waiters	500
Total fixed costs	**1,900**

With ticket prices at £10 it only needs to have 190 people buying tickets and it will have broken even. Every extra ticket it sells will be pure profit. The organisers consider the probability that 190 people will attend to be high, so the risk of this event is low. Any glasses of wine they sell will be profitable, as they make 50p profit on every glass sold. There is no risk attached to this. The financial risk they face is the fixed costs £1,900, so even though the risk that the event will not break even is low, they should consider whether they can afford to lose the amount of the fixed costs.

This is an example of using financial information to help in making a decision – whether to go ahead with the event. Often you are presented with choices – should we do this event or that event? Then the choice will be the event that shows the best return for the least risk. That is actually harder than it sounds, as return usually has to be reduced if you want a lower risk.

Consider:

- What is the downside if the event goes wrong? What are the fixed costs that will have been incurred before we can stop? Are these non-returnable?

- What is the probability that it will break even? This is easier to judge if you can convert the break-even target into some tangible measure, such as number of people attending.

The figures used in the example above do not necessarily represent the full cost of that fundraising event. The costs of the fundraiser's time (if a paid employee) and the associated overheads would need to be taken into account if you wanted to cost the fundraising event fully. However, that is not useful for decision-making. You are already committed to the fixed costs of the fundraiser and associated costs, so you have to live with those. You need to look at the financial consequences of your decision to hold the event.

Full cost recovery and overhead apportionment

Having established the different types of costs of the organisation and gained an understanding of the cost structure, you can move on to the difficult area of overhead apportionment. The objective of apportionment is to assess the full cost of an activity, so the basis of apportionment should be fair and reasonable. It should reflect the management time, administrative services, premises and other central costs utilised on that activity. The apportionment will have to be an estimate and is usually based on a measure such as:

- staff numbers

- staff costs

- number of clients

- amount of space used by department

- amount of income.

You may select different bases for apportionment for different overhead costs. For example, premises costs may be apportioned on the basis of space (square metreage), whereas telephone costs may be apportioned on the basis of staff numbers. Since staff costs are usually a very high proportion of an organisation's expenditure, this is most often used as the best indicator of the relative size of different activities, and therefore their relative use of central resources.

Understanding apportionment

Apportionment is obviously estimated and can never be an accurate assessment of the true cost of an activity. There is little point, therefore, in spending too much time in detailed calculations and data gathering to carry out the apportionment exercise. It is also not worth arguing over the basis of the apportionment for too long. Everyone in the organisation should be told how the apportionment is undertaken, but should also be reminded that you will not be taking decisions to cut activities on the basis of the budgets that show the apportionments. As discussed above, decisions will have to be based on different financial data. The budgets showing apportioned overheads are for the purpose of calculating the full cost of an activity. This is essential for fundraising purposes, and for identifying which activities generate surpluses and which require subsidy. All the central overheads have to be funded and the most common method is by apportioning them to projects, and thus including them in project funding applications.

Allocate direct costs

Apportionment will be less contentious if there are fewer costs included as overheads, and therefore a smaller amount is put down on each activity budget as overhead apportionment. It is better if you can identify more costs as direct and allocate these to the particular activity. For example, if a project is located in its own building, then it should be straightforward to budget and record the actual costs of the premises separately and allocate those costs directly to the project. You may decide to have a photocopier that requires a pass code before copies can be made, with a log being kept of the number of copies for each department or activity. This might work satisfactorily and should not involve too much extra work. However, trying to keep a log of each department's copies by having a paper and pencil next to the photocopier will probably be a waste of time. Somebody will have to spend time going through the figures, calculating the use by department and trying to reconcile it to the register of copies on the photocopier. An estimated apportionment would do just as well. You need to weigh up the value of the information against the effort required to gather it.

Funding applications

You need to understand the full costs of activities for internal budgeting, but also for funding bids. More and more funders will fund on the basis of full cost recovery, but you need to consider how you will present the information about your costs in funding applications. You may find it helpful to use the full cost recovery toolkit published by acevo (see *Sources of further information*). You will also have to consider any specific guidelines from funders.

The important thing to remember here is that a funding application is not the same thing as your own organisational budget. You should undertake the budgeting exercise for your own information and benefit, whereas funding applications should be prepared as a separate exercise, even though they will draw on the same information.

Presentation is the key, although you will, of course, also have to heed potential funders' guidelines on what they will or will not fund. Here are several options:

1. THE FUNDER STATES THAT IT WILL NOT FUND ANY OVERHEADS APPORTIONED TO A PROJECT You should therefore cost in *all* the incremental costs of that activity, including additional costs of telephone calls, installation and rental of a separate telephone line, if necessary, staff recruitment and every pencil and paperclip!

Taking on the new project will not provide a contribution towards the fixed costs of the organisation, but at least you should ensure that it is not a drain on resources. You may also wish to consider whether the new project will involve extra hours of central administration, as it may be possible to cost this in your funding application.

2. THE FUNDER QUESTIONS AN AMOUNT SHOWN IN YOUR FUNDING APPLICATION THAT RELATES TO THE OVERHEAD APPORTIONMENT One approach may be to explain what actual costs this relates to, by providing a brief outline of the organisation and how it is managed. For example, explain the staffing and management structure, the premises and how the organisation works. This is the rationale behind your budget and overhead apportionment method. Try to pre-empt the question from potential funders by providing these details in notes to your funding application.

3. THE FUNDER HAS A POLICY OF FUNDING A FIXED PERCENTAGE FOR ADMINISTRATION You need to be clear about what the funder will fund, and obtain clarification on what is included in the definition of administration and how the percentage should be calculated. Often it is a percentage of a project's direct costs. This approach forces you to identify as many direct costs as possible and prepare a more detailed budget than you might have done otherwise. You may be able to put some costs down as direct that you otherwise would have included in the overhead apportionment. For example, management of the project by the director or staff supervision may be allowed as a direct cost, even though it will in fact be an estimate and perhaps normally included in the overhead apportionment.

Cost centres

The overhead apportionment will be undertaken to spread costs over different cost centres. These will be departments or areas of activity, which can be easily identified as a logical way to split up costs. Cost centre budgeting will work best when there is a natural way to identify the cost centre, such as following the organisation's management structure. So if you have departments with managers in charge, it would be logical for them to have a cost centre budget to manage. Generally, the cost centres will be based on one of the following:

- geographical location, e.g. an area office
- services provided, e.g. membership services, trading operations
- internal departments or functions of the organisation, e.g. finance and administration, fundraising, education
- funding received from particular sources.

For charities, it also makes sense to bear in mind the Statement of Recommended Practice (SORP) when considering the appropriate cost centres. The SORP requires charitable expenditure to be analysed by activity on the face of the statement of financial activities (SoFA). It also requires the cost of generating funds to be analysed into relevant categories. This aspect of accounting is examined in more detail in Chapter 6. You may wish to check that you can easily convert your raw accounting information into final accounts that comply with the SORP.

Clearly, you will need to keep accounting records that will record actual transactions into the same cost centre structure. It is therefore wise to think about this aspect of the accounting process at the budgeting stage. You will need to be able to complete the bookkeeping for your cost centres without difficulty. For example, it should be possible to identify the direct costs of a cost centre without too much problem. It is usual to set up the organisation's central administration as another cost centre. This will hold all the central management costs and other costs, which are the overheads to be apportioned. You may want to split this into two (or more) cost centres if, for example, you decide to apportion premises costs on one basis and other costs on a different basis.

Example of allocation of central costs

Each area of activity has its own staff and some have volunteers. Additionally, there are some other costs, which can be identified as relating to a particular project. The Helpline operates from its own premises, but uses many of the other resources available centrally, such as stationery and postage. Some projects have their own computers and other equipment, so the budget heading for equipment is directly allocated where possible and includes depreciation as well as any maintenance costs.

Central costs include the salary of the director and support staff. All staff are recruited centrally, so the total costs of this are included in the central costs budget. Stationery is purchased centrally, although all projects use it.

Central costs are apportioned in two stages. Firstly, the premises costs are apportioned to all projects except the Helpline on the basis of space occupied. Secondly, all other overheads are apportioned on the basis of the staff costs of the project.

Calculations
For the premises apportionment, the space occupied was measured and the relevant percentage of the total calculated.

	Space occupied m²	% space	Premises costs £
Information	331	35%	8,750
Advocacy	189	20%	5,000
Newsletter	236	25%	6,250
Outreach	189	20%	5,000
Total	**945**	**100%**	**25,000**

For the other overheads, a similar calculation was undertaken, based on the staff costs of each project:

	Staff costs £	% staff	Other overheads £
Information	45,380	25%	19,446
Advocacy	23,577	13%	10,112
Newsletter	32,654	18%	14,001
Helpline	56,027	30%	23,336
Outreach	25,920	14%	10,890
Total	**183,558**	**100%**	**77,785**

Forecasting income

The income budget is usually more sensitive than the expenditure budget and subject to fluctuations and change. You will need to make assumptions in order to estimate future income. These should be noted down and the most important ones provided with the budget. The estimates will not make sense to anyone without explanation of the basis. Different types of income will need slightly different techniques for forecasting, but it should be possible to group income into categories of:

- confirmed/definite
- probable
- possible
- uncertain/target.

Confirmed or definite income will be when the source is known and the funds may already have been received. For example a grant or contract may have been awarded over three years, so the income for future years is certain. It may also be useful to include in the budget income that has already been received, for example as restricted funds (see Chapter 6), but remains unspent. This makes sense when you are trying to match income and expenditure into the same budget period.

Probable income will describe sources such as committed and direct debit donations, subscriptions and some grants and donations where the funder has indicated that the funds will be forthcoming. Some calculation may be necessary to arrive at a sensible forecast figure for the budget. For example, you have to assume that only a certain percentage of regular income from subscriptions or direct debit giving will be received because, for example, people may cancel or move banks. Past experience may help you to arrive at the percentage, which may be quite high (say 95 per cent of the amount of current subscribers), but you should also take into account activities to increase membership or regular giving.

You may also be using fundraising techniques such as raffles, direct mail or applications to companies and charitable trusts. If your charity has experience of a particular fundraising method, it may be reasonable to include an estimate of income under the category of probable. If your charity has no experience, then it is wiser to decrease the amount expected and push the income source into a lower category of 'possible' or 'hoped for'.

Possible income may include new sources of funds, or new funds from existing sources. So it may be that the charity is trying a new form of fundraising and it will have to estimate the amount it may receive. It usually takes some time to establish a new fundraising method, so the estimate in early budgets should be low. New fundraising methods can be included in this category where the plans have been made and it is definite that the fundraising effort will take place. This category can also include income from new members or new covenants where there is some planned activity to recruit new members or new donors.

Uncertain/target income will be appropriate for the unknown, but where the charity needs to find further funds. This may also include untried fundraising methods or fundraising for which there are no detailed plans. Obviously, one should not have too much income in this category!

Income budgets should be rooted in the fundraising plan, which should give full details of the costs and forecast income for each method of fundraising. The fundraising plan has to be achievable and should include reasonable estimates of forecast income. The targets set for fundraisers may not be suitable as the source for the income budget. It is more prudent to include a lower estimate of forecast income, to ensure there is not a deficit.

The timing of fundraising will be crucial to the financial stability of the organisation: this is examined more closely in the following section on cashflow forecasting. Some charities adopt a policy whereby they raise the funds first and then start the spending plan. This may not be possible for charities that are fundraising to fund current spending, but it is worth considering as a policy for the uncertain income in the fundraising plan.

Cashflow forecast

The revenue budget concentrates on the forecast income compared with expenditure, matching particular costs to the related source of funding. The budget will usually look at the overall figures for the year, arriving at a surplus or deficit. So the revenue budget may show that the organisation can break even over the year. In practice, however, the timing of cash inflows and outflows will not necessarily coincide. The cash position may be very bad at some points during the year, even though the position may improve by the year end. A cashflow forecast will help you to manage this aspect.

The cashflow forecast should be based on information in the budgets, but should forecast when actual receipts and payments will occur. In effect, you are predicting what your bank statements will look like. Usually, cashflow forecasts are prepared on a month by month basis for the forthcoming year. However, in times of crisis, you may plan cashflow weekly. In a period of expansion and change you may wish to extend the forecast period to 18 months, two years or even three years.

The cashflow forecast will include information from both the revenue and capital budget. It is concerned only with the actual cash flowing in and out of the organisation, not which budget heading it comes under. It will exclude depreciation, as this is a notional cost, not a cash payment. It will include the full price paid for new fixed assets acquired. It will include loans advanced or repaid, as well as receipts and payments, regardless of which financial year end they relate to.

Updating the cashflow forecast

The forecast is more useful if it is regularly updated. You may wish to change the forecast amounts to actual amounts when these become known, or insert an extra column alongside each month for actual receipts and payments. More importantly, though, you should review the future forecast figures and check that the amounts and timing still seem valid. You may have received better information and cashflow forecasts frequently need updating.

Interpreting the cashflow forecast

Your attention should be drawn to the 'bottom line' of the cashflow forecast. This tells you the forecast balance at the bank at the end of each month. If this is a negative figure, you are going to be overdrawn. If it is a positive figure, this is the estimate of cash balances available. Either way, you may need to take action. A general rule is to try to make the timing of cash outflows coincide with the timing of cash inflows.

If there are months when the cashflow forecast shows that you would go overdrawn, you may be able to look through the receipts and payments in more detail and see which could be brought forward or delayed. It is worth remembering that there is little point in delaying payment of a bill for £500 if the overdraft is going to be £5,000. You may lose the goodwill of a supplier and you will not necessarily avoid the overdraft by tinkering with several small amounts. It is better to look at the larger items and the 'structural' problems. Is the problem that you always estimate that income will come in earlier than it actually does?

Using the cashflow forecast – practical steps

1. Consider the various sources of income and put in appropriate descriptions as headings on left-hand side.

2. Try to group expenditure headings into fewer categories than are usually contained in a budget. For example, you could group together 'office overheads' rather than listing separately rent, rates, light, heat, insurance, stationery. You may know from experience that payments for all these work out to roughly £1,500 per month, so this would be sufficient. As long as no one item would severely distort the overall picture, then this would be sufficient detail.

3. Enter the amounts you expect to be receive or pay in the appropriate month on the appropriate line.

4. Total the receipts for each month (A).

5. Total the payments for each month (B).

6. Calculate the receipts minus payments for each month and enter the result in the monthly cashflow line. A negative result indicates higher payments out for the month than receipts for the month (A) − (B) = (C).

7. 'Balance brought forward' means the balance of cash at the bank at the beginning of the month (D). For the first month, this should be the figure from an agreed bank reconciliation (i.e. bank statement balance adjusted for known outstanding items). Note that you can draw up a cashflow forecast at any time during the year, not necessarily just for financial years.

8. Starting with the first month, you should sum the monthly cashflow figure with the balance brought forward. This will give you the balance to carry forward to go into the box on the line 'Balance carried forward (C) + (D) = (E).

Example – Cashflow forecast

	Months												
	1	2	3	4	5	6	7	8	9	10	11	12	TOTAL
Receipts													
Fees													
Donations													
Grants													
Investment income													
Loan advance received													
Total receipts	A												
Payments													
Net Salaries													
Inland Revenue													
Project costs													
Office costs													
Capital purchases													
Loan repayment													
Total payments	B												
Net cashflow for month	A–B=C												
Balance brought forward	D E												
Balance carried forward	C+D=E												

20

9. The balance to carry forward at the end of the first month is the balance brought forward in the next month, and so on.

Cashflow considerations

You need to know and understand the financial operation of your organisation well in order to plan the cashflow properly. Explore the following questions and consider the timing of activities to come up with a list of factors that will affect cashflow:

1. What are the historic patterns for receiving fundraising income?

2. How is earned income spread over the year?

3. When do we receive grants, bank interest, investment income, etc.? Do we receive this income in advance or in arrears?

4. Have we been realistic in forecasts of income from new projects?

5. Have we made an allowance for bad debts on earned income?

6. Have we included tax reclaims for gift aid in accordance with the expected timing of the claim and receipt?

7. Have we made allowances for staff changes and the time lag involved when recruiting new staff?

8. For new projects or developments, is there a lead time whilst the project is being set up with initial costs built in to cashflow?

9. Are payments for capital projects or new equipment included in the month when the expenditure is expected?

10. Does interest receivable or interest payable reasonably reflect the balance at the bank through the year?

VAT in cashflow forecasts

If the organisation is not registered for VAT, then all payments should be shown inclusive of VAT and income will not be affected. This is the same basis as for the budgets. If the organisation is registered for VAT, then receipts and payments should include VAT, but you will also need to prepare a little VAT calculation or estimate the amount of VAT that will have to be paid to or recovered from HM Revenue & Customs each quarter. VAT can have a significant effect on cashflow and so should not be ignored.

2 Financial reporting and monitoring

INTRODUCTION

Once budgets and forecasts have been agreed, it is essential to monitor them. For this reason, financial reports are a key management tool, both for the senior paid staff and the trustees. You will need to think about how different reports will be used by different people in the organisation. For example, the trustees do not need the same level of detail as a departmental manager. You should also consider the reporting timetable quite carefully, to ensure that information provided is recent enough to be useful.

BUDGET COMPARISON

The mainstay of management accounts is a comparison between the plan and the actual amounts recorded in the books. So the revenue budget should be compared with actual income and expenditure, for example. It is important that the comparison is a valid one, in other words that you are comparing like with like. Check that you are following a few simple rules:

1. The headings should be the same in the budget as in the accounting records. (There is no point in trying to compare a budget for stationery with actual expenditure for printing, postage and stationery.)

2. The time period should be the same (obviously, six months' budget should not be compared with seven months' actual).

3. The basis of the figures should be the same. (It is no good comparing total cash paid out on insurance premiums for a year with a budget figure of six months of insurance costs.)

Flexing budgets

You sometimes need to make adjustments to the basic budget figures in order to make valid comparisons. Seasonal variations or a development plan may mean that income and/or expenditure does not occur evenly throughout the year. It may be inappropriate to take a full year's budget and simply divide everything by two to create a budget for the first six months. Look at the situation of an expanding staff team, for example. You may have allowed for two extra staff in the second half of the year. Whilst this may be the equivalent of one staff member all year for the purpose of calculating the budget, a misleading impression could be given by comparing actual expenditure for the first six months with a simple half of the budget figure. So you should calculate the expected expenditure for the first six months and then compare actual expenditure for the first six months with that figure.

It is also possible to flex budgets in a slightly different way. Supposing you had prepared a budget on the basis of a plan that forecast a new project would come on-line in month four. The project implementation is delayed by three months. You can therefore flex the budget to take the project out; re-forecast, in effect. Then compare budget with actual and you must explain any further variations from the plan. By flexing the budget, you have removed one cause for differences.

If your income and expenditure has a seasonal pattern, then it may be wise to prepare budgets on a quarterly or even monthly basis. You then have a budget that is already flexed for the seasonal differences.

When working with committees, it can cause problems if the budget seems to be a 'moving target'. In this case, it may not be appropriate to present a flexed budget, but it is still a good idea to undertake the calculation as part of the variance analysis (see below).

Variance analysis

The difference between the budget and actual amounts of income and expenditure is known as a 'variance'. Significant variances need to be investigated and their cause identified. You should be able to analyse a variance by comparing the details of actual performance with the details of the original plan. The notes on assumptions underlying budget estimates will now be useful to help you analyse the financial information. Variances will most often be caused by one or several of the following:

- a change in price

- a change in volume

- a change in timing.

It is important to recognise the cause so that appropriate action can be taken. Is the variance reflecting a permanent increase in price, which means that the budget should be revised? Does a drop in volume (e.g. number of members) mean that income targets were far too optimistic and should be adjusted? Or is it just a delay and all will be well by the end of the year? Asking the right questions and carrying out the right sort of variance analysis will help groups take corrective action if necessary.

Example – Variance analysis

The budget showed membership income to be £11,690, whereas actual income is £10,300. To analyse the cause of the variance, we need to compare the variables separately:

a) rate of membership subscription

	Budget £	Actual £	Variance £
Individuals	18	20	2 (F)
Family	27	25	2 (A)
Junior	8	5	3 (A)

(F) = Favourable
(A) = Adverse

	Budgeted numbers	Actual rates £	£	Budget £	Variance £
Individuals	350	20	7,000	6,300	700 (F)
Family	170	25	4,250	4,590	340 (A)
Junior	100	5	500	800	300 (A)
					60 (F)

(b) numbers of members

	Budgeted numbers	Actual numbers	Variance numbers	Actual rates £	Variance £
Individuals	350	290	60 (A)	20	1,200 (A)
Family	170	150	20 (A)	25	500 (A)
Junior	100	150	50 (F)	5	250 (F)
					1,450 (A)

Total variance:

	£
due to rate change	60 (F)
due to volume change	1,450 (A)
	1,390 (A)

Much simpler variance analysis will be the norm, so it should be easy to provide explanations for variances in management reports. It is also useful to identify whether the variance is because of a permanent change, such as a price increase, or whether it is caused by a timing difference. A timing difference might be due to a delay in implementing a plan or because certain functions always happen at a certain time of year and your budget does not deal with seasonal differences. An example of a simple explanation of a variance would be as follows:

The budget forecast that 10 staff would be employed and that their salaries would be increased by four per cent for inflation. Actually, one person left half way through the year and the post was left vacant. The salary increase was actually three and a half per cent. Working this out in financial terms tests the validity of the explanation and demonstrates that you can explain the whole of the variance. So this example translates into numbers:

	£
Savings due to vacant post	7,728
Savings due to lower increase	513
Total variance	8,241

Monitoring key indicators

The whole management accounting process becomes much easier when you gain a full understanding of key factors in your organisation that affect financial management. Far too much time is wasted monitoring minor details that will make no significant difference to the organisation even if they do show a large variance. It is much better to think about the main drivers and focus attention on these. They may be obvious, but you may need to think about the consequences of things going wrong to pick them up. Some examples:

An organisation running training courses needs a certain number of people on each course in order to break even. So it needs a system that monitors the number of people registering on courses on a regular basis, even daily. This won't necessarily come from the financial accounting system, as this sort of information is likely to be on a database.

A key indicator for a housing charity will be the number of empty properties or beds, as it will only receive funding or fees for occupied spaces. Usually the empty spaces are valued at the rate that would have been received for them.

Some projects will be operating on a fixed expenditure budget, so for them the amount they are spending will be important. It may be more useful to know how much has been spent and how much has been committed by way of orders or decisions. The total then tells them how much of the budget allowance has been taken up and how much is left.

The format of management accounts should reflect the type of organisation and give due emphasis to the key indicators. This will probably mean that a lot less detail is included in management reports on fixed costs and overheads and other costs that do not vary a great deal, such as salaries. On the other hand, more attention may need to be given to cashflow items and monitoring cash balances, debtors and creditors.

Monitoring cashflow

Even charities with healthy cash balances should monitor their cashflow and liquidity. The focus of their attention might be to improve their treasury management, whereas a charity with limited resources may be focusing its cashflow monitoring on the ability to pay the creditors on time. The difference in emphasis may affect the method adopted for monitoring cashflow, but in fact the principles are the same.

The end of year balance sheet is a helpful starting point for assessing liquidity and it is essential that management accounts should include a balance sheet. This indicates at the very least that the accounts balance and gives some degree of reassurance on their accuracy and completeness, provided there is proper reconciliation of key balances in the balance sheet, such as the bank balances (see Chapter 5).

The balance sheet items under current assets and current liabilities will be of most interest in monitoring the cashflow and liquidity. These are the items that make up the working capital of the organisation. It is possible to assess an organisation's working capital needs by measuring the likely levels of the components under the following balance sheet headings.

Current assets

> Stock
> Debtors
> Loans to others
> Prepaid expenses
> Short–term investments
> Bank accounts
> Petty cash floats

Current liabilities

> Loans from others
> Bank overdrafts
> Amounts received in advance
> Trade creditors
> Accrued expenses

Tax and national insurance

VAT

For the purposes of management accounts, some of these headings will be less important than others. It will not usually be necessary to have very accurate figures for prepaid and accrued expenses, unless these are very significant. Similarly, the amounts received in advance do not have an impact on liquidity, as they will not have to be paid out, even though they are technically creditors. However, the cashflow forecast should show the expenditure on the projects for which the money has been received. Stock will be a key factor to be monitored if you are running a business, but not if it is a very minor part of your activities. Charities that carry a small stock of publications should not put a lot of time and effort into counting stock for management accounts.

From the balance sheet, you can then work forwards to a cashflow forecast, which predicts the cash inflows and outflows. My preference is for a cashflow forecast that combines all the bank accounts of the organisation, effectively treating them as one. Some people prefer to show only the current account on the cashflow forecast. Either way, the cashflow forecast should show the surplus funds or deficit at the end of each month. This should be reasonably accurate for a few months ahead. Appropriate action can then be taken to invest or to try to reschedule receipts/payments. As a last resort, loans or bank overdrafts may have to be sought, bearing in mind that this is the most expensive form of finance available. However, this may be necessary whilst fundraising plans are put into place and take effect.

Managing in a crisis

The cashflow forecast in this context is a management tool and a live document, needing regular updating to reflect changing circumstances. It is important that you date each version, so that you know which is the most recent. This is the management tool most needed by finance managers and chief executives in organisations experiencing cashflow difficulties. It will help with day-to-day decisions such as:

Which creditors should we pay today, this week, next week?

Can we afford a new piece of equipment?

Should we advertise this post or delay recruitment?

Can we delay other items of expenditure? Will this have any impact on income?

Cashflow is the key aspect of the finances, allowing you to monitor your organisation and to be aware as early as possible of potential financial difficulty. The examples below are typical mistakes.

Continuing to spend in accordance with an agreed budget, but ignoring the cashflow implications.

Using the brought forward reserves to fund expenditure – fine as a theoretical way of balancing a deficit budget, but a significant problem if the reserves do not exist in cash.

Spending on capital projects without monitoring this or planning adequately for the cashflow impact; this can happen easily in organisations where there is undue emphasis on monitoring revenue budgets.

Doing fundraising that requires large initial cash outlay. This is not the best type of fundraising for a charity that is short of funds.

Committing funds to fundraising with a long payback period, so that income will be slow to come in.

Managing cashflow in a crisis – action points

Exercise good credit control – chase debtors for prompt payment.

Review charging policies – can you ask for cash in advance instead of in arrears e.g. for book orders, subscriptions or services?

Bank receipts daily.

Ask major suppliers for special payment terms and stick to them.

Investigate payment of certain overheads by instalments, e.g. insurance, equipment maintenance.

Pay small bills promptly and avoid wasted time dealing with them.

Prioritise major payments.

Defer action that will lead to additional expenditure, such as recruitment, taking on leases, purchasing equipment.

If the organisation is in a cashflow crisis, it will need to consider four important points:

1. Can the organisation deal with the short-term consequences? Action on credit control, stock control and deferring expenditure may deal with the short-term problems.

2. Can the organisation come up with a long-term plan that will tackle the underlying problems? The reasons for the cashflow crisis may be complex and could, for example, relate to changed funding, underfunding of projects or core activities, an imbalance between the costs of administration and the amount of activity, historic overspending or excessive fixed costs, or failed initiatives.

3. In light of the answers to the above two questions, the organisation must consider whether it can continue its activities. If it is a limited company, the directors are bound by company law to cease trading when they can no longer pay their debts.

This means that they should not continue to commit expenditure when they do not know how they are going to pay for it. This includes paying out net salaries when the funds to pay the tax and national insurance are not available. Trustees of unincorporated charities also need to exercise care, because they will be personally liable to pay the debts of the charity if it becomes insolvent. This will include redundancy pay to staff where it applies.

4. If the charity has restricted funds (see Chapter 6) it must hold back the unspent restricted funds in cash to enable it to complete tasks required by the funding. All trustees have a duty to ensure restricted funds are used for the purpose for which they were given.

Using ratios

More and more charities are effectively running businesses, albeit charitable businesses. One therefore needs to consider any business methods that might be useful in monitoring the activities of the charity, including ratios and performance indicators. Ratios are more useful as a measure because they indicate the level of something or the rate at which something is done. In financial management, ratios can be used to indicate the level of money owed to an organisation and measure how quickly debt is collected. Here are a few suggestions for ratios that might be useful in setting targets and monitoring performance.

Aged debtor analysis

If you sell goods or services on credit, you will probably operate a sales ledger. If this is on a computerised accounts package, it will probably have the facility to produce a list of 'aged debtors'. This will analyse your debtors, showing month by month how much they owe according to the month in which they were invoiced. You can therefore see very easily from the totals how long the debts have been outstanding. Commonly the headings are current, one month old, two months old, three months old and over three months.

Whilst the aged debt analysis is useful for prompting action to collect debts, the calculation of a ratio will help you to see whether you are getting better or worse at debt collection. You can calculate the average number of days it takes the organisation to collect a debt, or 'days debtors', and check this on a regular basis:

$$\text{Total debtors} = \frac{\text{Days debtors}}{\text{Sales per day}}$$

There are several ways to calculate the sales per day; it does not matter which way you perform the calculation, as long as you are consistent. A fairly conventional way to calculate it is:

$$\text{Sales per day} = \frac{\text{turnover for year}}{365 \text{ days}}$$

For example, at the end of the month you may have £8,000 of debtors relating to unpaid invoices for services, the annual income from which is £48,000. So sales per day are £48,000 divided by 365 days = £131.51. The days debtors is calculated by dividing £8,000 by £131.51 = 61 days. So debtors are taking an average of 61 days to pay. Your invoice terms are 30 days, so debtors are, on average, taking a month longer to pay. This inevitably means that some people are taking even longer, so you need to think about credit control strategies. The effectiveness of those strategies can be monitored by checking the days debtors monthly. Note that ratios are useful because they describe the rate or proportion of something. The days debtors ratio tells us the proportion of sales which are uncontrolled debts. Even if sales increase, the proportion is still a constant measure.

Rent arrears

A variation on the debtors' ratio is a ratio that measures the amount of rent outstanding compared with the total rent receivable. This is usually expressed as a percentage of the number of weeks' rent the arrears represent on average. For example, rent arrears of £34,000 compared with total rent receivable for the year of £320,000 equates to 10.6%. Convert this into weeks by calculating the average rent receivable for one week (£320,000 divided by 52 weeks = £6,154) and then dividing the rent arrears figure by the weekly rent roll (£34,000 divided by £6,154 = 5.5 weeks). This means that, on average, tenants are five and a half weeks overdue with their rent. Targets can then be set and the arrears levels monitored through the ratio.

Occupancy rate – housing and residential care charities

Charities providing housing or residential care will need to monitor occupancy on a regular basis and usually do so by measuring the empty spaces or 'voids'. The voids rate is the percentage of voids compared with the total potential income. To make a valid comparison you need to value the voids at the rate of income that would have been receivable had the space been occupied.

For example, a hostel for young homeless people has spaces for 20 people each night and each space is normally eligible for funding of £10 per night. So total possible income for one week is $20 \times 7 \times £10 = £1,400$. The register shows that it had three empty spaces each night. The value of voids is therefore $3 \times 7 \times £10 = £210$. The rate of voids is £210 divided by £1,410 = 15%. The organisation can set itself a target in the budget for the level of voids, and monitor actual voids against this.

Return on fundraising

Business measures will be applicable to many fundraising efforts. An overall measure for comparing different fundraising methods and activities looks at the return the fundraising produces compared with the direct costs involved. For example, it might be possible to measure the return on a raffle by counting up the cost of the prizes, printing the tickets, sending out the tickets and any other direct costs (say this amounts to £3,000), then looking at the cash received for the sale of raffle tickets (say £15,000). The rate of return in relation to expenditure is therefore:

$$\frac{£15,000}{£3,000} \times 100 = 500\%$$

The expected rate of return for a particular type of fundraising will also help in setting budgets, as well as monitoring performance.

Cost/income ratio

Many commentators will compare a charity's income with the cost of its fundraising. Care is needed to ensure that this is a valid comparison. For management accounts, you would provide more accurate information if you produced return on fundraising information as described above for each main fundraising activity. However, senior managers and trustees may find it helpful to track the cost/income ratio during the year as a way of managing the likely financial position in the published accounts. Calculate the cost/income ratio by:

$$\frac{\text{Costs}}{\text{Income}} \times 100$$

Gross profit percentage

Gross profit percentage is a key ratio for many types of trade, such as retail selling of bought-in goods (not donated goods), mail order selling, Christmas card sales and other forms of merchandising. Calculate the gross profit percentage as follows:

$$\frac{\text{Gross profit}}{\text{Sales}} \times 100$$

Different rates of gross profit can be expected for different types of goods, but monitoring the percentage both overall and for individual lines will provide useful management information about performance.

Sales to space ratio

In retailing, it is usual to measure the takings compared with the amount of space occupied. This may be useful for comparing the performance of shops in different locations, as well as comparing performance from one week/month/year to the next. This is simply calculated by dividing takings by the number of square metres occupied.

PRESENTING YOUR INFORMATION

Graphs and pictures

Graphs and pictures can be a very useful way of presenting financial information; however, they need to be used appropriately. Graphs will focus attention on only one particular aspect at a time; pie charts that are cut into more than about four pieces become very difficult to read.

Graphs and pictures are best used in conjunction with some well-written text – they break up the text and highlight important aspects. Do not use graphs to excess or present graphs on some trivial matter, or your point will be lost. You also need to consider the right sort of graph for the type of information you are presenting. In general, people choose between pie charts, bar charts and line graphs for financial information.

Example – pie chart

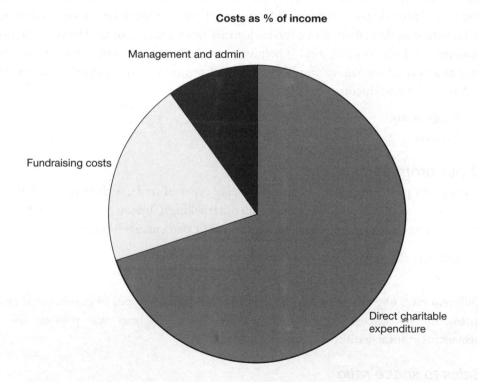

Costs as % of income

Management and admin

Fundraising costs

Direct charitable expenditure

Example – bar chart

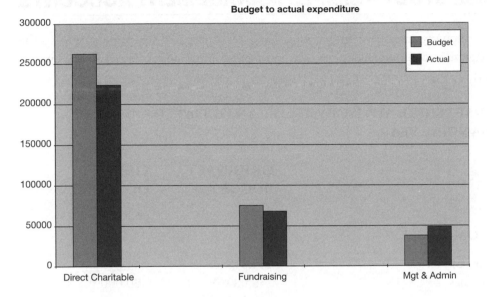

Budget to actual expenditure

Example – line chart

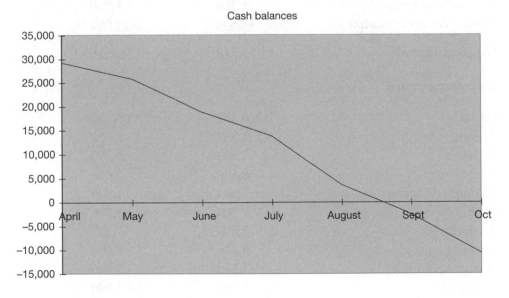

Cash balances

CASE STUDY – SIMPLE MANAGEMENT ACCOUNTS

The following management accounts have been prepared for presentation to the management committee. Look at the report and compile a list of good and bad points about it.

BORSETSHIRE ADVISORY TRUST ANTICIPATED OUTTURN FINANCIAL YEAR

	ORIGINAL BUDGET £	LIKELY OUTCOME £
INCOME		
Grants and fees	244,818	244,818
Shop sales	36,000	20,000
Donations	10,000	10,000
Fundraising	5,000	4,000
Bank deposit interest	1,700	1,700
Trading company receipts	18,000	18,000
(A)Total income	315,518	298,518
EXPENDITURE		
Salaries	220,362	205,593
Training	2,332	2,332
Travel	1,200	1,200
Recruitment	6,500	2,600
Volunteers' expenses	1,800	1,600
Publicity	2,500	2,500
Printing	7,500	7,500
Telephone	6,000	6,000
Postage	4,500	4,000
Stationery	3,500	2,500
Equipment	6,400	6,400
Accountancy/audit	8,000	9,725
Premises	28,885	30,000
(B)Total expenditure	299,479	281,950
Surplus/deficit (A–B)	16,039	16,568

BORSETSHIRE ADVISORY TRUST FINANCIAL YEAR

BUDGET TO ACTUAL FOR NINE MONTHS TO 31 DECEMBER

Key:

The variance shown is the difference between nine months' budget and nine months' actual.

Figures in brackets in the variance column mean that income is less or expenditure more (bad news).

Figures not in brackets mean that income is better or expenditure less (good news).

	Budget for year £	Budget for nine months £	Actual for nine months £	Variance £	Notes
INCOME					
Grants and fees	244,818	183,614	174,058	(9,556)	1
Shop sales	36,000	27,000	14,966	(12,034)	2
Donations	10,000	7,500	9,930	2,430	3
Fundraising	5,000	3,750	3,713	(37)	
Bank deposit interest	1,700	1,275	1,333	58	
Trading company receipts	18,000	13,500	6,878	(6,622)	4
Total Income	315,518	236,639	210,878	(25,761)	
EXPENDITURE					
Salaries	220,362	165,272	150,474	14,798	5
Training	2,332	1,749	2,332	(583)	
Travel	1,200	900	663	237	
Recruitment	6,500	4,875	1,301	3,574	6
Volunteers' expenses	1,800	1,350	803	547	
Publicity	2,500	1,875	1,213	662	
Printing	7,500	5,625	3,695	1,930	7
Telephone	6,000	4,500	4,624	(124)	
Postage	4,500	3,375	921	2,454	8
Stationery	3,500	2,625	1,526	1,099	9
Equipment	6,400	4,800	3,667	1,133	10
Accountancy/audit	8,000	6,000	1,725	4,275	11
Premises	28,885	21,664	6,674	14,990	12
Total expenditure	299,479	224,610	179,618	44,992	
Surplus/deficit	16,039	12,029	31,260	19,231	

BORSETSHIRE ADVISORY TRUST FINANCIAL YEAR

FINANCIAL MANAGEMENT REPORT UP TO 31 DECEMBER

Budget to actual for nine months – notes

The budget figures are the budget for the year as approved at the management committee on 13 February. These have then been apportioned to nine months by simply taking three-quarters of the annual figures. The *Actual for nine months* figures are the accruals basis income and expenditure figures prepared from the accounting records for the first nine months of the financial year.

Significant variances

The variance column shows the difference between the budget for nine months and the actual for nine months. The notes below explain the significant variances.

1. The grants income is less than expected because the council has not yet actioned the increased level of grant funding agreed verbally. We assume this will be paid in the final quarter, which is still outstanding.

2. Shop sales are much lower than expected. This seems to be due to over-optimistic budgeting and the long sickness of the shop co-ordinator, causing the shop to be open for shorter hours.

3. Donations are higher than expected for the nine months due to the legacy from one of the users who died last year. However, no further amounts are expected.

4. Trading company receipts are lower than expected because the transfers from the trading company have been delayed. A separate report to the trading sub-committee shows that net income should reach the budget for the year. A significant transfer will be made from the trading company before the end of March.

5. Salaries are lower than expected for two reasons. A) The pay increase was not implemented on time and this will have to be backdated. This will be put through payroll at the end of January and amounts to £3,456 including national insurance contributions. B) The post of advocacy co-ordinator has been vacant for three months and the post of administrative assistant has been vacant on and off for six months. The recruitment for a new advocacy co-ordinator has been undertaken and a new person will be in post at the beginning of February. The administrative assistant recruited earlier left because she found a better paid job and a new round of recruitment has commenced.

6. Recruitment costs are lower than expected as the personnel manager has changed the advertising policy and expensive adverts in national newspapers are no longer required. This will affect the budget for the year and projected expenditure on this item can be significantly reduced.

7. Printing costs are lower than expected, but this was due to a delay in the reprinting of a large number of forms and stationery items. This will now happen in the last quarter of the financial year.

8. Postage is low compared with budget because the petty cash expenditure was not analysed for these accounts, although a quick review suggests that this will be lower than budget anyway. This is probably because the budget was too high.

9. Stationery is underspent because the budget was too high. It is likely that printing and stationery budgets overlap and some costs have been budgeted twice.

10. Equipment includes maintenance and depreciation. The underspend may be used up by the end of the year.

11. Accountancy/audit includes the amount for the year end work, which will have to be accrued in the year end accounts, but the accrual is not in these management accounts. The actual expenditure relates to advice during the year, which was not budgeted.

12. Premises costs are under budget, because the council has not charged the correct amount of rent. We will have to accrue the full amount in the budget when we do the year end accounts, even if we do not know the actual rent to be charged.

Prepared by KS 14 January 2007

Case study analysis

Good points

■ The report states when it was prepared and by whom.

■ There is a key to explain the variances.

■ The budget to actual report for nine months also shows the budget for the year.

■ The likely outturn, in other words what the final figures are likely to be, is given.

■ There are notes to explain significant variances.

Bad points

There is no information on cash balances, debtors or creditors, and no balance sheet is provided.

Without a balance sheet, there is no information on the reserves (funds) levels of the organisation.

As it seems likely that no balance sheet has been prepared, this undermines the confidence we may have in these figures. This is indicated by the comment on postage; if the petty cash expenditure has not been analysed, where is the total spent through petty cash shown? Maybe the expenditure shown is incomplete in other ways.

Some accruals have been missed off, such as premises. The bad effect of this is counteracted by the provision of the likely outturn figures.

It would be better to show the likely outturn figures on the same page as the comparison between actual and budget.

There is no departmental or activity-based analysis of income and expenditure, so we do not know which areas are doing well or and which are doing badly. In particular, shop expenses and fundraising expenses are presumably included under other headings (e.g. printing, postage, stationery, premises), but they ought to be identified as separate departments, so that we can see the 'contribution' made by fundraising activities and the shop. (Contribution is direct income less direct expenses: see Chapter 1 for further explanation and examples.)

SUMMARY

Key points of good management accounts:

Recent – Each month's committee meeting should be presented with figures up to the end of the previous month; out of date management accounts have no value as management information.

Relevant – Attention must be focused on the key figures, and this is partly achieved by reducing the level of detail, so that questions like 'why are bank charges £10 over budget?' do not get asked. 'Less is more!'

Reliable – The completeness and accuracy of the accounting records should be ensured by monthly reconciliations. In addition, the preparation of a balance sheet as well as a statement of financial activities ensures that the management accounts have been correctly drawn from the accounting records. Reliability does not mean 100 per cent accuracy, since estimates have to be made in management accounts and speed will sometimes have to take priority over accuracy.

3 Financial controls and managing risk

It is important in any undertaking that proper control is exercised over the resources available. It is even more important for charities, because they handle public money and receive special tax benefits. Since trustees are responsible for ensuring that the charity uses all funds received for its charitable purposes, they should take a special interest in the establishment of proper systems and controls.

RISK

Like any other entity, charities are at risk of loss of funds or assets, or that funds will be misapplied. It may be helpful to consider the controls that are appropriate in most charities in the context of possible risks.

Broadly, there are two types of risk:

- Internal risk of fraud or mismanagement, which can be minimised by good controls and procedures.

- External risk of outside events affecting the organisation, usually in a detrimental way. This is outside the control of the organisation and management can only plan to mitigate the effects of any such events.

Internal risk

There is a higher risk of something going wrong internally in organisations where the control environment is weak. Some or all of the following could indicate this :

- Lack of formal or written procedures.

- Authority to commit the organisation rests with inappropriate people, usually individuals who are too junior and/or too inexperienced.

- Lack of reporting to the trustees, so paid staff are making all key decisions.

- Staff are not properly trained.

■ Trustees do not understand their responsibilities towards the charity's beneficiaries.

■ The wrong culture exists, for example a senior staff member treats the charity as if it were their own company and claims high travel and subsistence expenses or acts without the authority of the trustees.

■ Poor staff morale or personnel problems.

■ A dispute between trustees, or between staff and trustees, for example on the future course the organisation should take.

A poor control environment, as described above, may lead to fraud or financial malpractice. However, good financial controls are not just about preventing fraud; a lack of controls can also lead to expensive mistakes and unauthorised expenditure. A poor control environment should concern both staff and trustees; many cases have shown that when things go wrong, there are often allegations of fraud and malpractice. Every staff member and trustee should be able to rely on good controls, in the knowledge that this is also a form of protection for them.

Monitoring financial plans

One of the important ways in which trustees can exercise control over the affairs of a charity is through the planning cycle (see Chapter 1). It is essential that trustees approve the organisational budget before it is implemented. Once the budget has been approved, this is a mandate to staff to implement the plan. This will involve committing the organisation to costs, so it is important for staff that they have the authority for such expenditure.

The trustees can exercise significant control by monitoring the organisation's performance against budgets. They should receive regular reports that give them an overview of the financial state of the organisation and show comparisons of actual performance to budgets. Trustees should also ask for explanations of significant variances and recommendations for action (see Chapter 2).

Financial procedures

The other key aspect to internal financial control is to have adequate procedural checks. The trustees are responsible for ensuring that proper procedures exist and are implemented. One way for them to fulfil their duties is to require that a financial procedures manual is prepared. Whilst this will take time and effort, it can be undertaken gradually. Copies of memoranda and example forms can be accumulated and the notes built up section by section.

A manual will need regular updating and there is no point in insisting on difficult or time-consuming procedures that no one follows. It should be a practical guide for staff and trustees, useful for induction of new members and a source of reference for all.

Auditors will also be able to use it, and their time will be saved as they will not need to write so many systems notes. They should review the manual and comment or make any recommendations for changes. It is not adequate to adopt another organisation's financial procedures. No two organisations operate in quite the same way and the objective is to operate procedures that work.

Example: Financial procedures manual – contents

1. *Introduction* – How to use this manual.

2. *Organisation chart* – Who is responsible for what with respect to finances.

3. *Budget setting* – Timetable and responsibility for setting budgets. Suggested format and headings. Method of allocating overheads.

4. *Reports* – Frequency and type of report. Examples of format. Notes on how reports are prepared.

5. *Banks* – Details of bank accounts held and cheque signatories. Purpose or use of bank accounts if any are specific.

6. *Income* – Details of procedures for opening post, banking receipts, invoicing, handling cash and so on. Example forms.

7. *Expenditure* – Authorisation limits for approving expenditure. Procedures for large, unusual or one-off expenditure. System for approving and paying invoices.

8. *Payroll* – Procedures for documenting and communicating new staff appointments, staff leaving and changes in pay rates. Method of payment for staff and authorisation of payment.

9. *Petty cash* – Levels and types of expenditure that can go through petty cash. Who can authorise petty cash expenditure. How the system should be reimbursed and record-keeping.

10. *Staff expenses* – How expenses will be reimbursed: type and level of expenditure. Who can authorise staff expenses.

If you wish, the financial procedures manual can be more comprehensive and incorporate policy statements on areas such as reserves levels. The example given above is an outline manual; it is not comprehensive and could, if you prefer, be summarised into a few pages.

Internal controls

Procedures will only be effective if they incorporate adequate internal controls. These may be arithmetic checks or checks that something exists. Used together, the different internal controls should ensure that the accounting records are complete and accurate and the organisation's assets are properly looked after. The possible types of internal control are:

- physical

- arithmetical and accounting

- authorisation and approval

- segregation of duties

- supervision and training

- organisation and management.

PHYSICAL These are concerned mainly with safeguarding assets. Procedures should be designed so that access to assets is only permitted to authorised personnel. In other words, you need to keep equipment, cheque books and petty cash in safe places, preferably under lock and key. You also need to consider insurance cover in the event of fire or theft.

ARITHMETICAL AND ACCOUNTING Bookkeeping systems incorporate certain checks and balances, such as control accounts, trial balances and reconciliations. They also include systems such as sequential numbering of invoices so that their completeness can be confirmed. There should be checks that invoices and accounting records are correctly totalled and analysed.

AUTHORISATION AND APPROVAL All transactions should require authorisation or approval by an appropriate responsible person. Limits for authorisation should be set, so that minor items do not have to wait for the trustees' approval and major expenditure does not happen without their approval. The approval should always be documented, for example by a signature on a petty cash voucher or a minute of the trustees' meeting.

SEGREGATION OF DUTIES This is a way of organising the responsibilities for various aspects of a chain of events in such a way that different people provide a check on each other. It is not simply to prevent fraud, but also to provide a check to detect errors. Poor segregation of duties will allow one person to instigate, authorise and record a whole series of events that commits the organisation to significant expenditure. Good segregation of duties will separate out different aspects of the transaction, such as ordering, approval and payment, and ensure that different people have different roles at each stage.

Good segregation of duties can be difficult for small organisations, but they still need to consider this. It is quite reasonable to ask trustees to take a more active role if the charity has few staff. At its very simplest, the internal control system should separate the task of approving or authorising expenditure from recording of payments.

SUPERVISION AND TRAINING Any system of internal control will depend on the quality of the supervision and training of staff or volunteers. It will be up to the treasurer and senior staff to identify training needs and provide supervision and support to staff and/or volunteers undertaking finance tasks.

ORGANISATION AND MANAGEMENT The structure of an organisation – with reporting lines, budget holders, budgets and management accounts – should focus on the responsibilities of each post, not individuals, and should ensure that the right work gets done at the right level.

Implementing good internal controls

Some areas of internal control deserve special mention, as they can cause particular problems in charities.

POST OPENING CONTROLS In charities where a significant amount of unsolicited donations are received through the post – often in cash – it is essential to have robust post opening procedures. Unopened post should be kept securely, and when it is opened, two people should be present and a list made of all cash and cheques received. Someone else should bank the cash and cheques, preferably the same day. It will then be possible to check easily that all monies received were banked. There could be collusion between two staff to misappropriate incoming cheques, but this is rare. An additional measure would be to rotate staff, which would be appropriate where large amounts of cash and cheques are received by post.

CASH COLLECTIONS Collecting tins or boxes should be sealed and prenumbered, and a log kept recording the numbered tins sent to collectors. Two people should be present when the tins are opened and the cash should be banked as soon as possible

FIXED ASSETS Trustees must safeguard the assets of the charity and ensure they are used for the charitable objects. Equipment can be a difficult area to control, especially as trustees are not involved in the day-to-day running of the charity and therefore not physically present to ensure that assets are kept secure and properly used. It is therefore essential to have is a fixed assets register. This is an inventory or list of all the major items of equipment, showing when purchased, the cost, location and condition. Further details can be added, to make the list as useful as possible. For example, if there is a theft of property, it will be useful to have a record of serial numbers of equipment or other details for the insurers. You may also find it helpful to keep a note of the replacement cost, so you can assess the insurance cover needed, and to calculate and record depreciation on the register.

Having established a register, it is essential to make periodic checks; someone needs physically to check the existence and condition of the equipment and compare that with the information on the register.

CHEQUE PAYMENTS The signing of cheques is an important control in charities; the cheque signatory is authorising the withdrawal of funds from the bank for the purpose stated. It is usual for charities to require two signatures on every cheque but, in reality, this may be an ineffective control. The value of the control exercised by the second signatory will be lost if the individual just signs everything without actually checking it, or if they sign blank cheques in advance. It may therefore be better to consider carefully whom the cheque signatories should be, and allow one person to sign on their own up to a certain value.

For small charities, the trustees will have to be involved in signing cheques to a greater degree, as any other procedure compromises segregation of duties. It is better if the cheque signing can be organised into weekly or fortnightly batches, so that cheque signatories have a proper chance to look at the supporting invoices or other documentation before they sign. It is bad practice to ask signatories to sign a cheque as they are rushing out the door, or to sign incomplete cheques, for example where the payee details are not completed. Such situations can generally be avoided by planning ahead.

Make sure that cheques are made out to the full name of the payee; abbreviations can lead to fraud if the cheque gets stolen on its way to the recipient. For example, 'B. T.' can easily be changed to 'B. Thompson'. Make cheques for your telephone bill out to British Telecommunications plc.

Cheques do get lost and stolen in the post and it is therefore worth looking at other ways of paying people that avoid the postal system. The Banks Automated Clearing System (BACS), which transfers money directly from your bank account to the recipients' bank accounts, is available from all high street banks. You have to set up the account details of people you regularly pay, such as staff and suppliers, but you can then execute a whole batch of transactions with one set of signatures. As well as being more secure, it also saves time on writing out a large number of cheques. You need to contact your own bank about setting up this payment system. Most banks offer a similar service online.

STAFF COSTS For many charities, staff costs may be up to 80 per cent of total expenditure. Good controls here are essential, and should start at recruitment and selection. A job description and person specification should have been approved at the appropriate management level. There should be clear procedures for the selection process and these should be made known to everyone involved in recruitment.

References should always be sought, in writing and with a telephone call. This would identify a bogus reference, and is more likely to produce useful information where the previous employer has been reluctant to commit themselves on paper to the shortcomings of the potential employee. You may need to take up three references for certain staff involved in cash handling, as this is often a requirement of fidelity insurance policies.

Once an employee is in post, regular performance appraisals will assist the organisation to deal with problems and hopefully remove some of the causes of fraud. Fraud is often perpetrated by disgruntled employees or those with problems outside work. These situations may be prevented from developing by good supervision.

If the staff team is small and everyone works set hours, the monthly salary cost will be pretty stable, with a low risk of fraud or error. In larger organisations, or where staff are paid for hours worked, there need to be controls to ensure that payments are made at the proper rate, for work actually done. For example, in residential care charities, there is usually a staff rota which is planned in advance. Actual hours paid should broadly agree with the rota and variances should be explained. Obvious targets for fraudulent activity are false overtime claims, false timesheets and fictitious employees. The checking and authorisation of overtime claims and timesheets have to be taken seriously. Training may be needed for those responsible for this area.

CASH TRANSACTIONS Cash transactions are always more vulnerable to fraud and error and so should be avoided where at all possible. Since cash cannot be completely avoided, much stricter controls have to apply. Petty cash should be kept on a float (imprest) system, whereby it is topped up to a fixed amount. The cash drawn from the bank will not be a regular amount, but will represent the actual amount spent out of petty cash since the last top up. Do not use petty cash for inappropriate items. It should only be used for buying small sundry items, such as milk and supplies, cleaning materials, possibly stamps and small stationery items. Petty cash should only be topped up from the bank; keep any incoming cash separate and bank it intact.

Avoid paying salaries in cash. You may have to use cash to pay the cleaner and to reimburse volunteers' expenses, but ensure that the proper paperwork is maintained. The payment to the cleaner is still wages and should be considered part of the payroll. Volunteers should still be completing expense claim forms, even though they are reimbursed through petty cash.

EXPENSES CLAIM FORMS Staff and volunteer expenses is an area where charities need to exercise great care. There should be proper forms for claiming expenses and it is better to have separate forms for staff and volunteers. Expenses should be claimed regularly, say monthly. An appropriate person has to authorise the expenses as reasonable and necessary. The head of a department or project leader should authorise the expenses for staff in their teams; the chief executive would probably authorise the expenses of heads of department; the chair or treasurer will have to authorise the chief executive's expenses; the volunteer co-ordinator will probably authorise volunteers' expenses; and the chair and treasurer will have to authorise each other's expenses and those of other trustees.

Receipts should be attached to the expenses claims and adequate explanation given for why the expense was incurred. It is wise to have a written policy on the type of expenses which may be claimed and the amount that can be charged (for example mileage). Clear guidance at the outset may prevent many problems later.

EXPENSE FLOATS Staff may be given expense floats, but the float should be a reasonable amount. The float can only be topped up when evidence of expenditure is provided, which can be entered on the normal expenses claim. The float should be documented and staff should sign a form acknowledging receipt of the float. If they leave, they will have to repay the float, it should therefore not be too large. The staff float system can work in place of a petty cash system for small charities or small projects. It has two advantages: one person is accountable for it and there is no petty cash tin, often the target for thieves, on the premises.

CREDIT CARDS If staff use their own credit card for purchases they should claim reimbursement through the normal expense claim process. A company credit card scheme may be appropriate for charities where staff and trustees have to do a lot of travelling. Care must be taken, however, that proper expenses claims are still received from all individuals using the card. The temptation is to ignore the paperwork, as the bill gets paid anyway.

Example – implementing good internal controls

This example is for a small organisation, where segregation of duties is more difficult. There is only the director and administrator at the central office, all other employees are project staff.

1. Project leader prepares order for new equipment, at the same time confirming that this is within the budget for the project.

2. Director approves order and initials copy as evidence of approval.

3. Order sent by administrator.

4. Goods received at project. Project leader signs despatch note and passes it to administrator as evidence that goods have been received in good condition.

5. Administrator receives invoice from supplier and checks against despatch note and copy purchase order and checks arithmetical accuracy of invoice, initialling invoice and coding to correct project and budget heading.

6. Administrator prepares cheque and cheque payment form, and presents with invoice to cheque signatories.

7. Cheque signatories sign cheque, thus authorising the disbursement of funds from the organisation's bank account. They also initial the cheque payment form.

8. Administrator enters cheque payment in the cash book, analysing according to budget heading and project code.

9. Administrator prepares a bank reconciliation at the month end.

10. Treasurer reviews the bank reconciliations and once a quarter checks that they have been properly prepared.

Internal risks relating to law and regulations

Charities are subject to charity law, of course, but there are many other laws that apply equally to charities as to any other entity. Care must be taken that the charity's procedures incorporate checks and controls to ensure that they comply with the law as it applies to that particular charity and its area of operation. Breach of the law will frequently cost the charity a great deal in penalties or damages. Examples of areas where problems frequently arise are given below:

■ PAYE legislation requires an employer to deduct tax and national insurance and pay it to HM Revenue& Customs (HMRC) for all employees. Not applying the PAYE procedures to casual employees and sessionals/consultants when HMRC considers that these people should have been on the payroll will result in significant liabilities. Similarly, paying volunteers in a way that jeopardises their volunteer status will cause PAYE problems.

■ Health and safety regulations apply to a large number of charities and you must ensure that you have complied with the regulations.

- Employment law is changing quickly and charities are frequently taken to employment tribunals. The costs of mistakes in this area are high, so it will be cheaper to get proper advice on employment issues at the outset.

- Restricted funds must be spent in accordance with the donor's stated wishes. Charities must ensure that their procedures identify incoming restricted funds and then apply proper checks that the funds are spent appropriately. Trustees may be personally liable for a breach of trust.

- VAT registration is compulsory if the organisation goes over the registration threshold, with penalties for late registration. Penalties are also due if large mistakes are made and found on an inspection visit. Charities need to ensure that they take appropriate advice on VAT issues (see Chapter 10).

- Charities may find themselves inadvertently trading, especially when undertaking new types of fundraising (see Chapter 9). This could lead to tax liabilities and censure by the Charity Commission. Proper advice is needed before embarking on new ventures.

Internal audit

Internal audit is one of the ways trustees can ensure that proper procedures are in place. Internal auditors will also look for improvements in efficiency and economy, looking into all the operations of the charity, not just the finance function. Only large organisations can afford to employ full-time internal auditors, but some charities purchase an internal audit service and others use volunteers to undertake certain tasks that are part of an internal audit programme.

In considering areas for internal audit, you need to think about the risk profile of the different aspects of the charity's operations. Areas of high risk will be targeted first and will be subject to more rigorous checks. The risk profile will be an assessment of the likelihood of various events taking place, together with the consequences to the charity if they do. This should not be restricted to purely financial events. For example, petty cash floats are vulnerable to theft, and this may cost the charity a few hundred pounds over a year. However, a serious incident which harms a child in the care of an employee of the charity might irreparably damage the charity's reputation and consequently its ability to fundraise. Which is the more important risk to guard against?

AUDIT COMMITTEE The internal audit team should have a clear line of reporting to an independent body of people, usually the audit committee. The audit committee should be made up of a few trustees and other non-executive people, possibly co-opted for their technical expertise in this area. An internal audit will not be sufficiently independent if it only reports to the finance director or chief executive. It should ultimately report to the audit committee, which will also be responsible for agreeing the priorities for internal audit attention and the programme of work for each cycle. Clearly, senior management do need to be involved in the internal audit process, but they should not be allowed to control or block it.

Risk of insolvency

A major concern for trustees is the risk of insolvency, especially where they are held personally liable for any outstanding debts. Trustee indemnity insurance will not usually cover the risk of insolvency.

LIMITED LIABILITY Only companies and industrial and provident societies give members limited liability. This means that the individual trustees/directors are protected financially if the organisation goes bankrupt, although they can still be held liable if they were negligent in any way, for example by allowing the charity's assets to be used for purposes outside the charitable objects. The trustees of a trust, charity or unincorporated association will be personally liable for the debts of the organisation if the charity has insufficient funds to pay them. This could be a significant amount if the charity has paid staff, who are entitled to redundancy, or if there are other contractual obligations such as a premises lease. Once a charity has significant contractual obligations it would be appropriate for it to consider incorporation, and therefore the benefits of limited liability. If a charity knows that it intends to employ staff or take on premises, then it is wise to choose an incorporated structure from the outset.

Incorporation means that the organisation is a separate legal entity and only the assets of the charity, not individual trustees or directors, are at risk if the charity goes bankrupt.

INCORPORATING A CHARITY Many charities begin as an unincorporated association or trust and then decide later that they wish to enjoy the benefits of limited liability. It is not possible to convert an existing charity as such; the process involves setting up a new charity and transferring the old charity's assets and liabilities to the new one. This also means a new charity number, new bank accounts and, inevitably, new stationery, so it can be an expensive and time-consuming process. It can be more convenient from a financial perspective to time the changeover to coincide with the end of the financial year. The new charitable company must have been set up and registered with the Charity Commission in advance.

Since a new company must have its first financial year end more than six months but less than 18 months after incorporation, it should be possible to keep the same year end after the changeover. You will need to submit final accounts for the old charity to the Charity Commission showing a nil balance sheet after the transfer of assets and liabilities to the new charity.

It is not possible to incorporate a charity with net liabilities. The trustees of the new charity would not be allowed to accept the liabilities, as to settle these from new monies may not be applying the funds to the charitable objects. Additionally, the creditors of the old charity are protected in this instance and the trustees of the old charity do not escape their personal liability by incorporating.

Incorporation may help trustees to sleep at night, but it does not mean that one can then ignore the risk of insolvency. Good practice in financial management means that you exercise budgetary control and monitor the financial position of the organisation on a regular basis. Insolvency rarely happens overnight and the organisation should be able to see the warning signs early. The trustees then have to weigh the benefits of the various options available to them and act in the interests of the beneficiaries.

External risks

External risks are those events over which the organisation has no control. Examples include:

  loss of funding

  fire, flood, landslide or any other natural disaster.

  legal actions

  changes in political environment

  changes in legislation

  market forces.

In responding to these threats, you have to consider strategies to mitigate your losses, because you cannot stop the event itself. The response will obviously vary, depending on the nature of the threat.

Diversifying income
Many charities are dependent on one major source of funding in their early years; as the charities mature, they usually try to spread the range of their funding sources. This is a way of spreading risk, so that the loss of one source of funding does not then mean closure of the charity.

Managing fixed costs
Organisations that would be significantly affected by external changes in the political and legislative environment should consider maintaining their flexibility by keeping their fixed costs down. For example, campaigning groups need to be able to respond quickly to new events. This will be easier if they can gear up to larger-scale activity

for a short while, and then scale down again. Maintaining a large infrastructure all the time will be costly and may lose them support. High fixed costs will also be a problem for organisations dependent on a few sources of funding. If you have built up the central administration of an organisation to cope with projects that only have three-year funding, you must have a strategy for dealing with the wind-down to a smaller infrastructure after that funding ceases.

Scenario planning

Having contingency plans for possible future events that may threaten the organisation can prepare you to handle an external risk. Working through some 'what if . . .?' questions and thinking through the consequences may also affect your plans and help you ensure that the threat does not affect you too much.

Insurance

Some external risks can be covered by insurance. Employer's liability insurance is compulsory for organisations with paid staff (and advisable for those with volunteers only) and organisations should have insurance against the risk of fire, theft and flooding. In fact, there may be other areas to consider for insurance, for example, if your organisation gives advice, you may want to cover it in the event of a legal action being brought against you for negligent advice. Organisations should always check the terms of the cover carefully and review all insurance annually. Cover needs to be adequate and cover the organisation's risks.

Time period of commitments

It is unwise to commit the organisation to long-term expenditure when there is a risk that it may not have long-term funding. Lease commitments for equipment and premises may tie the organisation into committed expenditure for periods that go beyond the horizon for funding. When an organisation is young and the external threats to its existence real, it would be better to minimise these types of commitments.

Reserves policies

The objective of having unrestricted funds in reserve is to enable the charity to cope with unplanned events. Very often, the effects of the event can be managed in the long term, but in the meantime the charity needs reserves. There is no rule on how large reserves should be; this will depend a great deal on the nature of the charity's activities and the level of external risk perceived by the trustees. It will also depend on what other action the charity is taking to mitigate the effects of the external threats. For example, a charity with high fixed costs will need high levels of reserves in order to cope with the effect of a reduction in income. Another charity might take action to reduce the level of fixed costs and will not then need such high levels of reserves.

Separate company

A separate company, which may be charitable or not, depending on its objects, could be set up to undertake some of the activities of the organisation, particularly trading. This is a way of mitigating the effect of failure of one area of activity on the rest of the organisation. Some charities have set up separate companies to undertake contract work to ensure that charitable reserves are not used to support the contract activity in the event of problems. This might be a useful strategy to deal with certain types of external risk, but it is not a substitute for proper assessment of the risk of the new venture. If the venture is too risky to undertake in the main part of the charity, then one has to consider whether it is too risky to undertake at all.

SUMMARY

Many of the controls necessary for the proper management of a charity often seem to create extra administration costs, so some charities try to skimp in these areas. Whilst it is quite right to endeavour to keep administrative costs to a minimum, this should not be done at the expense of good financial controls. Internal controls and regular review of external risks will help to ensure the safety of the charity's funds and its ability to fulfil its objects.

Common control weaknesses and how to avoid them

1. *The payee details on cheques may be the initials of the charity.* If the cheque falls into the wrong hands, the payee could be amended to an individual's name. For example, a cheque made out to B.T.C could be altered to B.T. Collier. It is therefore wise to have a rubber stamp with the full charity name on it, which can be used to complete the payee details properly.

2. *Purchase invoices could be presented twice for payment, without the cheque signatory necessarily noticing.* This can be a deliberate technique for defrauding an organisation, as the second cheque to the supplier is diverted into another bank account. Purchase invoices should be cancelled with a rubber stamp PAID or in a similar way.

3. *Copies of purchase invoices are presented for payment.* Copy invoices could be duplicates, or they could be invoices to another organisation with the details changed, which can be done relatively easily on photocopies. Payment should never be made on copy invoices, only original ones.

4. *Payment is made to a supplier on the basis of a statement, without the original invoices.* This may lead to payments being duplicated and should therefore be avoided.

5. *A dummy supplier could be set up, or a friend could be set up to send in dummy invoices.* The check on despatch notes should help to eliminate some of these, if segregation of duties is operated properly. However, special care may be needed when the invoice relates to services (rather than goods), where no despatch note is received. The person approving the invoice for payment should be considering whether the services have actually been received.

6. *A relative of a member of staff or a trustee undertakes building improvements for the organisation or provides computer consultancy or other services.* Whilst they may be providing services on fair terms, this might be in doubt unless they won the contract on a competitive basis – how will the organisation know it is getting value for money? Contract services need to be properly ordered and a tender procedure followed where the amount involved is significant. This usually means that at least three potential contractors are asked to tender. This will apply to building work, but also consultancy work and other types of services. If a tender is not appropriate, then the terms and conditions should be stated in a letter of appointment, setting out the expectations of the contractor.

7. *Cash is drawn from the bank to purchase items of equipment from retail stores, because the retailers will not accept a company cheque.* It is usually possible to arrange for cheque payment on the day of purchase, or the goods can be purchased on a pro-forma invoice. The supplier will release the goods once the cheque has cleared. Another option is to give a staff member a float (making out a cheque to them personally, rather than cash) and make them accountable for the use of the funds. They have to provide a breakdown of all expenditure on a claim form and provide all receipts. This may be appropriate when the charity is moving to new offices or starting a new project.

4 Investment

DUTIES OF TRUSTEES

Charity trustees have a duty of care to the charity's beneficiaries in all their areas of responsibility, but this is particularly brought into focus when it comes to investing the charity's assets. The Trustee Act 2000 sets out the trustees' duty to maximise the value of assets and therefore to invest them to obtain a good return. However, they should not risk losing the assets by investing in highly speculative, high-risk ventures. Charity trustees must balance risk against return.

Trustees must also balance the future needs of the charity against the current needs. They should therefore consider whether the maximisation of income for current use is in the best interest of future beneficiaries i.e. will it mean a loss of capital growth and hence income growth? Trustees need to balance long-term capital growth against income generation.

Capital growth should, at the very least, be sufficient for assets to maintain their value compared with inflation. In practice, most investment advisers are trying to beat inflation and obtain much better capital growth as well as producing some income. The balance between how these two factors are struck will therefore depend on whether the priority is for income generation or capital growth.

A total return approach to investing aims to maximise the overall investment return, rather than specifying the amount expected in the form of income and the amount expected in the form of capital gain. The capital gains, dividends and interest are pooled.

Historically, charities with a permanent endowment have had to allocate capital returns to the permanent endowment fund, and investment income generated was available for distribution as unrestricted funds. In 2001, the Charity Commission issued new operational guidance, which allows permanently endowed charities to apply for permission to operate a total returns approach to investment. The charity may then allocate some of the capital gains to distributable income.

Trustees' considerations

When investing the charity's assets the trustees should consider the following:

- Whether the charity's investments are sufficiently diversified. This means that the charity should not put all its eggs into one basket and risk losing a large part of its assets on any one investment.

- Whether the investments are suitable for the charity. This refers to the need for a charity to consider what are suitable investments for its size, the amount to be invested and the period over which it wishes to invest.

- Whether a particular investment vehicle is suitable as one of its kind. This means that trustees should consider whether the particular investment is too risky or speculative, or is in any other way inappropriate.

Ethical investment

Particular attention has been drawn to the duties of the trustees in respect of ethical investment through various court cases. One of the better known cases was brought by the Bishop of Oxford against the Church Commissioners in 1991. The case was that the Church Commissioners should not be investing in certain types of companies, including those that were active in the defence industry and in South Africa (this was at a time when apartheid was still being actively pursued as a policy in South Africa). The argument was that such investments were contrary to the Christian ethic. The Bishop did not win the case, because the Judge ruled that the trustees' first consideration must be to maximise the return on investments. Trustees can take ethical considerations into account, but this should be because they are in the interest of the beneficiaries, not the trustees' personal values.

It may be appropriate for certain charities to avoid certain activities when considering their investment criteria, because such investment would be in conflict with their charitable objects. For example, a cancer charity may wish to avoid investment in the tobacco industry. This is justifiable, because clearly the promotion of smoking is contrary to the charity's objects and not in the interests of the charity's beneficiaries.

Since the ruling in the above-mentioned case, more funds have been set up to reflect the public interest in ethical investment, and charities may wish to look at these as possible investment vehicles. However, trustees should take care to examine the return on their investment carefully. There should be no problem if the ethical fund produces a return that can be expected to be at least as good as the return on another fund.

Programme-related investment

This is also known as 'mission-related investment'. A number of charities are finding ways of making part of their investment portfolio available for their charitable objectives. For example, instead of holding shares and distributing the income to community groups through grants, a charity could buy a building for community groups. This transaction would be part of the charity's charitable activities rather than its investment activities. Thus the building would be shown within the balance sheet under tangible fixed assets, and any rental income would be an incoming resource from charitable activity.

Powers to invest

The Trustee Act 2000 came into force on 1 February 2001. It applies to all charities set up as trusts or unincorporated associations, but not to charitable companies. The Act sets out a new general power of investment, which allows a trustee to place funds in any kind of investment, excluding land, as though he or she is the owner of those funds. There is also now a separate power to acquire land as an investment.

If the governing document restricts powers of investment, then this restriction or exclusion will still apply. The investment powers for charitable companies will be set out in the memorandum and articles of association, but these are generally widely drawn, to include most investments.

For charities now covered by the Trustee Act 2000, this new general power of investment is wider than that previously allowed (under the Trustee Investments Act 1961). You will need to ensure that the existing portfolio is appropriate, given these wider powers.

Investment policy

Every charity should draw up an investment policy, even if it has only small sums to invest. Even placing funds on deposit at the bank is a form of investment. There is an overlap here with the charity's reserves policy, which will need to be clear first. The trustees are not directly achieving the charitable objects by investment of the funds; they will be producing income or increasing the capital of the charity, which may then be applied to the charitable objects.

The investment policy should look at several points, including the following:

- Does the charity need to generate income from the investment, or is the priority to maximise capital growth?

- Does the charity need access to the funds at short notice? Can some funds be identified as available for long-term investment?

- What risk is the charity prepared to accept and what is permitted under the charity's investment powers? How should the charity diversify its investment portfolio in order to minimise the overall risk of loss to the charity?

■ Are there any ethical considerations to which the charity can legitimately pay heed?

■ For long-term investment, is there a preference for a managed portfolio of investments, unit trusts or common investment funds?

A charity with an endowment fund may find it relatively easy to work out its investment policy, whereas a charity that only has surplus working capital may need to undertake its financial planning first. The outline cashflow forecast for at least the next two years will be needed in order to draw up the investment policy. Having been drawn up, an investment policy must be kept under review. The trustees should review it at least once a year, but also if there is a significant change in circumstances or a sudden new influx of funds, such as a legacy.

TYPES OF INVESTMENT

Trustees have to make choices about the type of investment they think is appropriate. Most charities will look to stocks and shares (either directly or indirectly, through pooled funds) for their investment choices, although where permitted they may also consider property. The risk profile, time horizon and likely returns will determine whether the type of investment is suitable for a charity. Trustees will also need to consider their investment objectives to assess whether the type of investment is suitable for the position of their particular charity. Generally, the options available to charities are as described below.

A deposit account with a bank or building society. These accounts usually offer immediate access, or they may be on seven days' notice, or other notice periods. The rates of interest will usually increase as the amount invested and the notice period increase. Charities should still consider the risk of placing large sums with one bank or building society. Although one can consider really big high street banks to be almost risk-free, this cannot be said for some of the smaller financial institutions. Recent banking collapses should serve as a warning that things can go wrong and depositors can lose their money. One should be wary about interest rates that seem to be very high compared with other banks; if the return seems too good to be true, then it probably is! As a precaution, charities should establish whether the bank is a member of a deposit protection scheme. Regulations came into force on 1 July 1995 ensuring that compensation of 90 per cent of the sum deposited, up to a maximum of £20,000, would be paid to depositors in the event of a default by the bank or building society.

A common deposit fund is a special deposit fund available only to charities in England and Wales. The fund, which is itself a charity, is a system of pooling cash deposits from many charities so that the amount available for investment is increased and the return improved. The fund manager will invest the pooled fund with several banks or deposit takers, so the risk is spread. They are often investing overnight or for a day at a time, offering easy access to funds. Interest is paid gross, so the whole sum is immediately available without the necessity for tax repayment claims. Some managers even provide a cheque book with this type of account.

Equities are the shares of companies. Companies pay out dividends on their shares, usually twice a year, although there can be no guarantee about the size of the dividend. The market value of the shares can go up or down, but mostly one is looking for capital growth as well as dividend income. The risk of investing in equities can be reduced by spreading the investments across a portfolio of shares in different companies. The risk can also be reduced by choosing blue chip companies – the top UK companies with a good track record of paying out dividends and capital growth. Investing in foreign companies quoted on overseas stock exchanges is usually perceived as being higher risk.

Gilts are fixed interest securities, such as government stocks. These include loan stocks, bonds, debentures and preference shares issued by central and local government and companies. They are known as gilt-edged securities, hence gilts, because the rate of return is fixed and the risk of loss of capital is low. The rate of return is low compared with equities, and capital growth is unlikely. Most balanced portfolios include some gilts as a way of balancing the risk profile of the other elements. National Savings Bonds are a form of gilt and are often used by charities with small amounts to invest where they cannot afford to risk their investment. The return should compare with a deposit account, but there may be a penalty if you sell before the maturity date, thus making these unsuitable if you may need to access the funds at short notice.

A unit trust is a pooled investment fund that invests in quoted shares. These will be wider-range investments and often specialise in a certain area; alternatively you can choose a general trust. The past performance of different unit trust funds can be examined to help in the choice, but this will not necessarily guarantee future performance. This is a form of investing in a portfolio of gilts and equities that is more diversified than could be achieved by a charity with a relatively small amount to invest. However, they involve fund manager's charges or commissions and you should find out what these are when comparing different unit trusts. Many unit trusts charge entry and exit fees, in addition to annual management fees. There is no guarantee on either the income or the capital of these funds.

Common investment funds are pooled funds similar in many ways to unit trusts, but with additional benefits for charities. Common investment funds (CIFs) are approved by the Charity Commission and registered as charities. An independent board of trustees determines the fund's investment policy and the trustees have the same responsibility as any charity trustee to maximise returns within the constraints of reasonable risk. The advantage of CIFs is that they are spreading risk, because the pooled funds are invested in a range of stocks and shares. These are tax-free and therefore carry the advantage of paying out income gross. In addition, the administration charges tend to be much lower than for ordinary unit trusts.

Property will only be a suitable investment for charities with large funds available for investment and the power within their governing instrument to buy property. It will also only be suitable as a small proportion of the total portfolio. Property is a long-term investment and cannot usually be sold quickly should the charity need access to the funds. Specialist advice will be needed to help trustees assess the prospects for capital growth and risks associated with returns. They may also need to consider the costs involved in managing and maintaining the property. It is not appropriate for trustees to speculate in land deals or to enter into development deals, as the returns for the cash investment are highly variable.

Derivatives are generally contracts for a deal at a future date, which are bought and sold in the hope that a profit can be made. They include futures, options, interest rate swaps and foreign currency deposits. These are highly speculative and the risk of loss is high, whilst the probability of a high return is quite low. They are not suitable for charities and are best left to the traders in the market. Charities may wish to buy foreign currency as a future deal if they know they have a future commitment and wish to fix the exchange rate of that transaction. This is a legitimate use of derivatives and is not speculative, rather it is hedging the risk of foreign exchange rate movements in the period before the foreign currency is needed.

Works of art are not usually used by charities as an investment vehicle, nor do governing instruments generally permit it, as there is no income or certainty of capital growth and an investor has to be able to wait until the market conditions are right for a sale. This is different from charities buying such items in fulfilment of their charitable objectives, in which case a purchase would not be classified as an investment.

Size of investment

Before embarking on an investment strategy, trustees need to decide whether they have enough to invest. Because of transaction costs, and entry and exit costs for certain investment vehicles such as unit trusts, it is uneconomic to buy and sell shares over short periods. You therefore need to be fairly sure that the funds you invest can be left intact for a reasonable period and will not be needed at short notice.

You will also need to have a reasonable sum to make the exercise worthwhile. It will not be worthwhile setting up a portfolio with a fund manager unless you have at least £500,000 – £1 million. The Charity Commission advises CIFs for charities with funds of less than £1 million.

Working capital

Trustees need to leave sufficient working capital available at fairly short notice for the immediate needs of the trust and some contingencies. Careful monitoring of the cashflow should inform the trustees over a period how much is likely to be needed in working capital. You would have to take into account planned changes and fundraising activities. It may be useful to think about the working capital needed in terms of a number of months of running costs. For example, a charity running services and paying salaries will need to think about how long it is committed to those costs. From this exercise, the trustees may decide that they need to keep at least three months' salaries and running costs immediately available, with a further three months' working capital available at three months' notice. The balance of funds could be invested, maintaining some flexibility within the portfolio for access to some funds at fairly short notice.

Treasury management

The trustees can still exercise good treasury management over the funds held for working capital. This also applies to trusts that do not have large funds and therefore do not plan to invest in the longer term. This involves cashflow forecasting and monitoring of the funds necessary for day-to-day finances. Only funds immediately needed should be held in a current account, with additional funds held on deposit. Banks offer a range of options for the best management of day-to-day funds and this should be discussed with the charity's bank manager. Common deposit funds will also be available. You need to keep the situation under review, as interest rates change and the types of deposit accounts available vary.

Investing in stocks and shares

If the trustees decide they have sufficient funds to invest in stocks and shares, they need to consider how this is to be managed. There are a number of options:

- **Direct management** of a portfolio of stocks and shares. Trustees who are suitably qualified could directly buy and sell their own stocks and shares. This still has to be undertaken through a stockbroker, although a share shop could be used. Transaction costs are kept down, but trustees could be vulnerable if there was a fall in value in the portfolio, since they would not be able to show that they had taken appropriate advice.

- **Advisory management** means that the trustees obtain advice on the selection of investments, but make the decision on the actual buying and selling of investments themselves. The financial adviser can be an appropriately qualified trustee or employee, although this can cause some problems if the portfolio falls in value. Consequently, many charities consider it more appropriate to obtain independent advice in investment matters. If a firm of fund managers is used, then it will usually buy and sell as nominee holder of the shares and deal with all the administration. This is a significant advantage as the administration can be onerous if equity shares are held over a period, due to matters such as scrip issues, rights issues, takeovers and mergers.

■ *A discretionary portfolio* involves an investment manager managing investments on behalf of the trustees. The charity would have to pay the investment manager's fees for this service and the portfolio would be balanced to ensure that risk is spread. In order to get the necessary diversification, this option is only suitable for charities with very large funds to invest (probably at least £1 million).

■ *A common investment fund* would be more suitable for those with smaller amounts to invest. Advice should be sought on a suitable fund, although trustees might be able to interpret the comparative data on the performance of various CIFs published regularly in *Charity Finance*. The funds are approved and are currently monitored by the Charity Commission, and because they operate like unit trusts, the risk is spread over a portfolio of investments held by the fund. Additional advantages are that the income is received gross, CIFs have independent trustees and they are cost-effective.

Appointing an investment manager

Under the Trustee Act 2000, trustees have the power to employ agents to manage the charity's assets. There should be a written agreement with such agents and their performance should be kept under review.

Custodian trustees

There can be practical problems for unincorporated charities in holding shares, and more particularly transferring shares. This arises because the charity is not a legal entity itself and therefore cannot own property; the trustees must hold the shares on behalf of the charity. This problem can be avoided by the use of custodian trustees, a nominee company or incorporation of the governing body.

A custodian trustee is a corporate body authorised to hold investments or land on behalf of others, for which they make a charge. It only acts as the nominated holder and does not manage or take over the liabilities. The investments belong to the charity and the trustees are responsible for them. The charity trustees have to instruct the custodian trustee before the latter can take any action in respect of the investments.

THE OFFICIAL CUSTODIAN FOR CHARITIES This was a free service established under the 1960 Charities Act, which was vastly reduced under the 1993 Charities Act. The official custodian used to hold investments on behalf of charity trustees, receive and pay dividends to trustees gross of tax, inform trustees about rights issues and so on. The official custodian was not an investment adviser, however. Under the Charities Act 1993, the official custodian passed back all holdings in stocks and shares to the charity trustees themselves.

The official custodian may still hold land on behalf of charities and will hold other investments in certain circumstances, for example where it is considered that the charity's property needs to be protected.

NOMINEE COMPANIES Investment managers frequently have nominee companies for holding the legal title to investments for their charity clients. Charities may only take advantage of this service if their trust deed or constitution expressly allows it or the Charity Commission makes an order authorising it.

INCORPORATION OF THE GOVERNING BODY Although the trust or organisation remains unincorporated, the trustee body is incorporated and may therefore hold the title to investments. This avoids the situation where individual trustees have to put their names forward for the purposes of holding investments or executing other legal documents.

SUMMARY

Trustees need to consider their investment policy and investment strategy carefully, taking advice where appropriate. Investment strategies will vary depending on the amount available to the charity to invest, but small charities should still consider their policy in this area, as they still have a duty to maximise the return on the charity's assets.

5 Accounting basics

ACCOUNTING RECORDS

Good financial records are the basis for sound financial management of your organisation. All organisations need to keep records of their transactions so that they can access information about their financial position. This information is retrospective, but keeping good records will help you to plan better for the future. It is worth spending some time thinking about the information you will need, so that you can keep your records in sufficient detail. You need to know how much the organisation has received over a specific period, but you also need to know the type and sources of income. You can then use this information, for example, to determine the effectiveness of a fundraising strategy.

Legal requirements for accounting records

All charities are required by law to keep adequate accounting records. Section 41 of the Charities Act 1993 extends the provisions set out in the Charities Act 1960 in relation to the maintenance of accounting records:

■ Charities must keep accounting records to show and explain the charity's transactions.

■ The accounting records should contain day-to-day entries for all sums of money received or spent, showing the source or destination of funds.

■ Charities must keep records of assets and liabilities.

■ Trustees should be able to show with reasonable accuracy the charity's financial position on any particular date in the past.

■ Accounting records must be kept for at least six years after the end of the financial year to which they relate.

The above applies to all unincorporated charities; charitable companies are covered by similar requirements in company legislation.

Simple accounting records

If the charity is small, there is no need to keep complicated books. For many charities, an analysed cash book will be adequate as the main accounting record. This is a simple, day by day record of receipts and payments analysed under various headings. The headings should coincide with the budget headings, for example rent, postage, stationery (see example analysed cash book at the end of this chapter). A straightforward filing system can support the entries made in the book – a lever arch file for payments, with invoices filed in cheque number order is sufficient. A folder for holding invoices awaiting payment would deal with creditors. Similarly, good filing systems can deal with controls needed for receipts.

Minimum accounting records

At the very least, every charity should have the following:

- Cash book for each bank account (for example current and deposit accounts).

- File for paid invoices, keeping them in date order of payment, marking on them date paid, cheque number and by whom approved.

- Folder for unpaid invoices.

- File for income-related correspondence or remittance advices.

- Filing systems for correspondence relating to grants and donations from regular funders.

- Petty cash book.

- File or envelopes for petty cash vouchers.

Keeping accounts records

Cash book

The cash book records all the entries going through the bank account. If you have more than one bank account, you should keep a separate cash book for each. The purpose of the book is to keep a record of all the transactions going through the bank in greater detail than the bank statement will provide and identify at any one time the balance of money in the bank. It is also used to analyse the receipts and payments into appropriate headings. You can maintain your cash book using an electronic spreadsheet, a handwritten book or accounting software.

Receipts (taken from the paying in book) are usually written on the left-hand side and the details recorded as follows:

Date

Reference (e.g. paying in slip no.)

Payee

Amount – in total

Amount – analysed under the appropriate headings

Payments (taken from the cheque book stubs) are normally written on the right-hand side in cheque number order. Standing orders may be entered from standing order forms (it is a good idea to have a master list of all your standing orders, showing frequency, amount and payee).

Bank reconciliation

The cash book must be kept up to date and reconciled regularly to the bank statement to ensure that the organisation's records are complete and accurate. The bank reconciliation will also highlight any errors made by the bank. If bank reconciliations are performed at the end of each month, the cash book will be an accurate, complete and up-to-date record of receipts and payments. A sample form is included in this chapter.

Bank reconciliations are normally performed monthly, as follows:

Obtain bank statement for period

Check items from cash book and tick off against bank statement

Enter bank statement balance at end of month

List payments not yet presented (i.e. not yet cleared on the bank statement)

List income not yet credited

Calculate adjusted bank balance

Enter in the cash book any items of expenditure on the bank statement not already in the cash book (e.g. standing orders, bank charges)

Enter in the cash book any items of income on the bank statement not already in the cash book (e.g. direct credits, bank interest)

Enter cash book balance at end of previous month

Enter total receipts and payments for the month

Calculate adjusted cash book balance, which should agree with the adjusted bank balances

Petty cash book

The petty cash book records all the entries going through the petty cash tin. If your organisation has more than one location, you may wish to provide more than one petty cash tin; a petty cash book should be kept for each.

The cash going into the tin should always come from the bank, i.e. you go to the bank and draw on a cheque. If you receive cash it should be banked intact and not put into the petty cash tin. This is very important because it ensures that a proper control over cash can be exercised.

You should decide on an amount for the petty cash float, say £100 or £250, depending on the expected level of expenditure.

THE IMPREST SYSTEM Having drawn an initial cheque for cash of say £100, all subsequent amounts drawn should equal the amount of expenditure and therefore top up the float so that it consists of £100 cash again. When people draw money from the petty cash tin they should use petty cash vouchers. Effectively, the cash to top up should always be exchanged for vouchers to the same value. This is the imprest system.

An advantage of this system is that, at any time you count the money and vouchers in the tin, they should always add up to £100. If they do not, then someone may have forgotten to put in a voucher or taken the wrong change.

When you top up the float take out the old vouchers as you put the money in. The vouchers are used as the source information for writing up the petty cash book and so it is essential that they are complete. Vouchers should be kept in a file.

The petty cash book will look similar to the cash book but is normally smaller because the expenditure is only on a few budget headings. As in the cash book, you need to enter the total amount of the voucher in the total column and then use the columns extending to the right to analyse the expenditure under appropriate headings. When you total all the columns you have a summary of how that amount of petty cash was spent.

NON-IMPREST SYSTEMS An alternative to the imprest system is to draw cash from the bank in round sums as required. Expenditure from petty cash is entered in the petty cash book from the vouchers, as above, and totalled regularly (normally monthly). A control account should also be performed regularly.

Daily banking sheet

If the organisation receives more than a few cheques a week, it should consider daily banking. In addition, a proper record of cash and cheques received should be made at the time the post is opened (this should be undertaken with two people present). An example sheet is included in this chapter, which can be adapted if you only bank on a weekly basis. If this sheet is used, the totals from the sheet can be entered into the receipts side of the cash book, rather than repeating all the same information. This streamlines the record keeping and saves time. You will need to keep the sheets in a file in date order, as they form part of the receipts record.

Expenses claim form

Staff and volunteers may need to be reimbursed for expenses incurred on behalf of the organisation, such as travel, accommodation or small purchases. It is better to use proper expenses claim forms (see example in this chapter) for this purpose, rather than petty cash vouchers. Receipts for the expenses can be stapled to the back of the form as further evidence for the expense incurred. This ensures that proper authorisation for these expenses is obtained, whereas using petty cash can circumvent such controls.

This is important for proper administration of the payroll. A compliance visit from HM Revenue & Customs will usually include a check on petty cash, looking for cash payments to casuals, staff or volunteers. The form included in this chapter can be adapted to your own organisation. It is advisable to create separate forms for staff and volunteers, especially as the rules for reimbursement and authorisation are usually different for each of these two categories.

It is possible to pay the reimbursements through the petty cash system, but the expenses claim form, rather than petty cash vouchers, should still be used as documentation.

Full bookkeeping systems

Nominal ledger

Full bookkeeping systems use a nominal ledger. This is a central record which pulls together the basic bookkeeping information. The nominal ledger is like a series of pigeon holes and you can use it to sort basic information. You will need to feed information from your working account books (cash book, petty cash book, sales and purchase ledgers) into the nominal ledger. It allows for records to contain information about cost centres (i.e. the different departments or projects under which costs fall), and is therefore a better basis for preparing accounts, particularly if your organisation grows or becomes more complex. You should also consider setting up a nominal ledger when the organisation has several projects or a number of funders, each requiring different reports. It will also help to set up appropriate systems prior to computerising accounts (see Chapter 8).

A nominal ledger will contain a page for each account heading (rent, stationery, equipment, salaries, telephone etc.), which should include all the different types of receipts and payments, as well as all assets and liabilities. It is similar to a card index system; in effect, when you write up the nominal ledger from the cash books or other day books you are sorting information into appropriate pigeon holes.

Other elements in a full bookkeeping system may include:

■ sales ledger and sales day book

■ purchase ledger and purchase day book

■ stock ledger.

These, together with the cash books, are the day-to-day working accounts books.

It is possible to set up a nominal ledger without the additional ledgers; the choice will depend on the activities of your organisation. If you have a significant amount of sales on credit, then you will need to keep track of the amounts owed to the organisation, so in this case a sales ledger is advisable. In a similar way, the decision to set up a purchase ledger will depend on the volume of purchase invoices. A purchase ledger is not necessary if you only have a few purchases and usually pay these promptly. If you can manage with just a folder for unpaid invoices, then this is probably adequate.

Having completed all the entries for a particular period, it is then possible to list all the balances on each account. This is known as a 'trial balance' and is the starting point for the preparation of accounts if you keep a nominal ledger. From the trial balance, you will need to sort the balances into those which are assets, liabilities, incoming or expended resources. You then make the adjustments for accruals, prepayments, depreciation and so on, as described below.

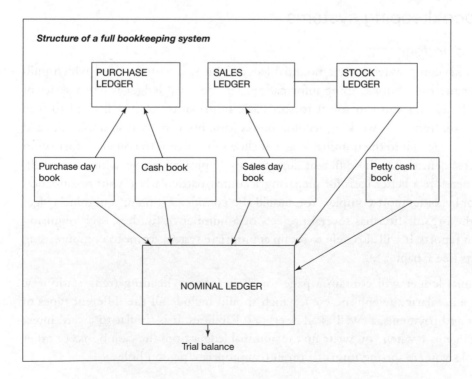

Structure of a full bookkeeping system

PREPARING ACCOUNTS

Accounts need to take into consideration not only the receipts and payments for a particular period, but also the assets and liabilities. Adjustments will have been made to reflect any outstanding unpaid bills and prepaid expenses at the end of the financial year. Receipts and payments are the starting point for the preparation of accounts, but you will need to make the necessary adjustments so that your final statement of financial activities shows the whole picture for the year. The adjustments are the loose ends which will be incorporated into the end of year balance sheet and picked up at the beginning of the next financial year.

If you do not keep a nominal ledger, the accounts preparation process can be done from the cash books.

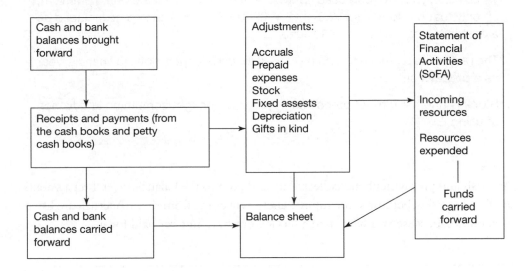

Accruals and prepayments

To ensure that the accounts reflect the actual incoming resources and expenditure for a particular period, adjustments have to be made to allow for timing differences between the cash transaction and the financial period to which it should belong. It is for this reason that the accounts will not always reflect the cash book totals for the financial year. The preparation of accounts starts with the receipts and payments, but then adjusts those amounts to produce incoming resources and expenditure, matching up accruals and prepayments into the correct financial years.

Accrual – example

Your financial year ends on 31 March. In May you receive an electricity bill for £450 which covers three months' use, from 2 February to 1 May.

One month's usage of electricity is estimated at £150. February and March usage ought to be included in the accounts for the financial year up to 31 March, so an accrual (i.e. record of the debt) for electricity of £300 needs to be included in the costs for the financial year ending 31 March.

Prepayment – example

Your financial year ends on 30 June, but you paid an insurance premium of £900 for one year's cover on 15 April.

By 30 June, you have only used up two and a half months of the year's premium, so only that proportion (i.e. 2.5 ÷ 12 × £900 = £187.50) should be included as a cost in the accounts up to 30 June.

The rest of the premium should be carried forward to the following financial year as a prepayment.

Stock is another form of prepayment; you have bought something in advance of using it.

Accruals and prepayments are collected up and go into the balance sheet. Prepayments are listed as assets, because some future benefit will come from them. Accruals are listed as liabilities, because you have used a service but have not yet paid for it.

Where to look for accruals:	**Where to look for prepayments:**
Rent	Insurance
Rates	Computer maintenance
Electricity	Rent
Gas	Rates
Telephone	Subscriptions
Audit fees	Training

Depreciation

Depreciation is a way of recognising that fixed assets such as equipment lose value and suffer wear and tear. This is another cost to the organisation, which needs to be accounted for. It can only be estimated, you will therefore need to explain how depreciation is estimated in your notes to the accounts. In this way, readers of accounts can come to their own conclusion about whether the basis of the estimate is reasonable.

Depreciation – example 1

Your organisation is expanding and opening a shop to sell bought-in goods to visitors. The cost of fitting out the shop is £10,000. This money has been spent in anticipation that it will help to produce future income. You will need to estimate how long you think the equipment will last and therefore how long it will generate income. If you estimate this period to be five years, then the depreciation is £10,000 over five years = £2,000 a year.

In other words, the estimated cost of the wear and tear on the equipment and shop fittings is £2,000 a year over five years. This is more reasonable than trying to recover the whole cost of fitting out in year one.

Depreciation is allowed on fixed assets such as equipment and vehicles. The actual purchase cost of such items is treated differently from other payments, for example bills, salaries and rent. Expenditure on fixed assets is separated out and put into the balance sheet. It will not appear as a single cost on your SoFA; instead, the yearly depreciation cost appears over several years.

Depreciation – example 2

Your organisation buys a minibus, which is used to transport older people on visits to day centres. The minibus costs £32,000 and you estimate that it will have a useful life of four years. Its yearly depreciation will be £8,000. This will appear in the balance sheet as:

Balance sheet
End of Year 1 (Extract)

	£
Fixed asset – cost	32,000
Depreciation to date	(8,000)
Net book value	24,000

Balance sheet
End of Year 2 (Extract)

Fixed asset – cost	32,000
Depreciation to date	(16,000)
Net book value	16,000

Balance sheet
End of Year 3 (Extract)

Fixed asset – cost	32,000
Depreciation to date	(24,000)
Net book value	8,000

Balance sheet
End of Year 4 (Extract)

Fixed asset – cost	32,000
Depreciation to date	(32,000)
Net book value	Nil

Depreciation for each year appears as an expenditure item, as well as reducing the value of the fixed assets.

At the end of an asset's estimated useful life it will have a nil net book value. This does not necessarily mean that it is unusable, simply that further use is a bonus. If the estimated useful life of an asset changes, you could consider changing the yearly depreciation, however this is not necessary unless the effect on the accounts is significant.

Accounting for gifts in kind

Donated equipment should be included in the accounts by showing the value to the charity under 'donations'. The same amount will then be treated as a fixed asset and depreciated accordingly. It is in effect as if someone had given you the cash and you had bought the asset. In a similar way, any donated goods should be brought into the accounts. However, charities selling donated goods in shops will only need to record the proceeds of the sale as a donation, rather than having to value the goods. Also, charities receiving donated goods for distribution usually only bring these into the accounts at the time of distribution.

SUMMARY

Good accounting records will help in the sound management of the organisation. Those records will need to be more extensive as the organisation grows and will need to cope with the complex funding of most charities. Bookkeeping involves the maintenance of the accounting records, which may include a nominal ledger and other ledgers. Accounts preparation is more than bookkeeping, being the preparation of a statement of financial activities and balance sheet, taking into account the various adjustments needed.

Example – Cash book receipts

Date	Ref	Total	Fees	Mem'ship	Donations	Grants	Other	Notes
April								
1 Local authority	R/345	25,000.00				25,000.00		
3 Whitbread	R/346	2,000.00			2,000.00			
3 Collection	R/347	3,089.45			3,089.45			
4 April membership	R/348	4,050.00		4,050.00				
5 Insurance claim	R/349	1,018.76					1,018.76	
5 DSC – courses	R/350	850.00	850.00					
13 DSC – consultancy	R/351	500.00	500.00					
15 BT Community Fund	R/352	1,000.00			1,000.00			
17 Refund – training fee	R/353	105.00					105.00	
20 Anonymous donation	R/354	100.00			100.00			
24 Sponsored swim	R/355	756.42			756.42			
28 BBC appearance fee	R/356	70.00	70.00					
TOTAL		38,539.63	1,420.00	4,050.00	6,945.87	25,000.00	1,123.76	

Example – Cash book payments

Date	Ref	Total	Salaries	Phone Post, Fax	Stat'y	Premises	Training	Sub/ Pub	Sundry	Travel
April										
1 Landlord – rent	Chq 367	2,345.00				2,345.00				
1 Voluntary Service Council	Chq 368	70.00					70.00			
3 Stamps	Chq 369	100.00		100.00						
4 NCVO	Chq 370	110.00						110.00		
5 Local authority – rates	D/D	93.80				93.80				
8 Dudley	Chq 371	264.92			264.92					
15 British Telecom	Chq 372	458.03		458.03						
18 Inland Revenue	Chq 373	2,964.84	2,964.84							
20 Net pay	BACS	6,917.96	6,917.96							
22 Petty cash	Chq 374	97.64		15.00	3.45			35.00	44.19	
25 Legal & General	Chq 375	960.35	960.35							
26 Staff expenses	BACS	306.42			21.15			14.00	23.75	247.52
30 British Telecom – fax	Chq 376	108.92		108.92						
TOTAL		14,797.88	9,882.80	681.95	289.52	2,438.80	70.00	159.00	1,028.29	247.52

Example – Petty cash book

RECEIPTS			PAYMENTS								
Date	*Cheque*	*Amount*	*Date*	*Details*	*Voucher*	*Total*	*Postage*	*Stat'y*	*Pubs*	*Provisions*	*Cleaning*
April			April								
			2	Stamps	PCV143	5.00	5.00				
			3	Folders	PCV144	1.23		1.23			
			4	Milk	PCV145	6.70				6.70	
			6	Cleaning materials	PCV146	3.67					3.67
			8	Reference book	PCV147	35.00			35.00		
			11	Milk	PCV148	6.70				6.70	
			13	Stamps	PCV149	5.00	5.00				
			15	Tape	PCV150	2.22		2.22			
			18	Milk	PCV151	6.70				6.70	
			19	Cleaning materials	PCV152	7.84					7.84
			20	Tea, coffee etc.	PCV153	5.88				5.88	
			21	Milk	PCV154	6.70				6.70	
22	Chq 374	97.64	22	Stamps	PCV155	5.00	5.00				
				TOTAL		97.64	15.00	3.45	35.00	32.68	11.51

Example – Expenses claim form

Name.................................. Month..........................

Date	Reason/nature of expense	Total	Travel	Stat'y	Phone	Sub/Pub	Provisions	Other
TOTAL								

Claimed by...........................(Signature)   Approved..........................(Signature)

.............................(Date)

Example – Bank reconciliation   Prepared by.....................   Date.................

Adjustments to bank statement balance:

Balance per bank statement at................   £

Less:
Unpresented cheques
Cheque no.   £

Total   £

Add: Outstanding credits
Pay in slip no.   £

Total   £

Adjusted bank balance

(These adjustments will clear next month)

Adjustments to cash book balance:

Balance brought forward in cash book   £

Add: Receipts in month
Less: Payments in month

Balance carried forward
Less: expenditure on bank statement, not in cash book (For example, bank charges)

Add: income on bank statement, not in cash book

Adjusted cash book balance

(Write these adjustments into your cash book)

Example – Daily banking sheet

Analysis:

Chq/Cash	Received from	Receipt No.	£	Grants	Donations	Subs	Other

TOTAL   ——— ———— ———— ———— ————

PAYING IN SLIP NO............................

PAID IN TO BANK BY............................

                     Initials   Date

ENTERED NOMINAL LEDGER.............

                     Initials   Date

6 Charity annual accounts and audit

The Charities Act 1993 initially introduced the legal framework for the audit and accounts of unincorporated charities. This has been updated by the Charities Act 2006, which is being implemented in stages in 2007 and 2008. Charitable companies refer to company legislation for determining whether a statutory audit is required. This legislation was also updated with the Companies Act 2006, which is also being implemented in stages. There are exemptions from audit for small charities, with changes being introduced in 2007 and 2008 as explained in more detail below. The format of the accounts for all charities is guided by the *Statement of Recommended Practice: Accounting by Charities* (SORP), issued by the Charity Commission in conjunction with the Accounting Standards Board.

THE FORM OF CHARITY ACCOUNTS

The SORP is regularly updated and a revised version was issued in March 2005. This is commonly referred to as SORP 2005. The revised version applies to accounting periods commencing on or after 1 April 2005. It contains guidance on the suitable treatment and presentation of charity accounts and represents good practice. The SORP applies to all charities, except for small charities and a few instances where there is a more specialised SORP, such as higher education institutions and registered social landlords. Small charities with income below £100,000 may choose to prepare a receipts and payments account. The most important points in the SORP are explained below.

No profit

The SORP tries to get away from the concept of profit as the measure of success or failure. The profit concept is not appropriate to charities, as charity law requires them to use all funds to further the charitable objects. The profit and loss account (income and expenditure account) is therefore replaced by a statement of financial activities

(SoFA). The SoFA brings together all the resources available to the charity and shows how these have been used to fulfil the charity's objectives. For example, incoming resources will include new endowments received by the charity, even though these are new capital to the charity. Donated assets and services are also brought into a SoFA, whereas commercial profit and loss accounts would not include them.

Incoming resources

Charities should show all incoming resources in the accounts in the year in which they arise, under suitable categories. Where possible, charities are encouraged to link incoming resources to related expenditure through the use of appropriate headings. The main categories for incoming resources in the SORP are:

- Incoming resources from generated funds:

    - voluntary income

    - activities for generating funds

    - investment income

- Incoming resources from charitable activities

- Other incoming resources

Which income goes in which category?

- Voluntary income – grants, legacies and donations freely given for the general purposes of the charity, typically general donations from individuals and trusts.

- Activities to generate funds – trading and fundraising such as charity shops, fundraising events and the sale of Christmas cards and merchandise.

- Investment income – bank interest, dividends on shares held, income from fixed interest securities, rental income from property held as an investment.

- Incoming resources from charitable activities – fees or grants received specifically to deliver services or activities.

- Other incoming resources – unusual items such as the proceeds from the sale of fixed assets.

Charities may use headings that are appropriate to describe their activities: it is not obligatory to use the exact words of the headings in the SORP. Charities are encouraged to use sub-headings to describe the activities in a way that people will readily understand and link to the narrative in the trustees' annual report. It is also common practice for the details of sources of funding to be included in the notes to the accounts, for example details of grant funders, although this is not required under the SORP.

Resources expended

Normal accounting concepts apply to the recognition of expenditure for charities, with expenditure incurred before the end of the financial year included in the resources expended for that financial year. Resources expended are split into three main activity categories, being:

- costs of generating funds

- costs of charitable activities

- governance costs.

COSTS OF GENERATING FUNDS The costs of generating funds are the costs involved in obtaining funds for the charity's work, such as advertising, direct mail, staff time, an agent's fees. It can include obtaining donations, but also sales of goods or services if the purpose is to raise funds, such as the sale of Christmas cards.

The costs should be broken down to match the headings used in incoming resources. So fundraising costs should be analysed between:

- costs of raising voluntary income

- costs of activities for generating funds

- investment management costs.

The costs of generating funds should *not* include any costs associated with delivering charitable activities, nor the costs of negotiating funding for such services. These costs will be included within the charitable activity to which they relate.

Information targeted at potential donors (rather than potential beneficiaries) should be part of the costs of generating funds, even where it provides general information about the charity's activities. So publicity to raise the charity's profile should be included in this category, but not advertising to promote the charity's objects or to educate people about the cause. For example, advertising to recruit volunteers or new pupils to a school should be seen as part of the charitable activities of the charity. Advertising a jumble sale to raise funds would be part of the costs of generating funds. Publicity to promote the charity's objects is likely to be targeted at beneficiaries or others who can use the information to further the charity's objectives.

Fundraising costs should not be netted off against income. Where a subsidiary company is used to undertake some of the charity's fundraising activities, the costs of those activities would have to be included under the costs of generating funds in the consolidated SoFA.

COSTS OF CHARITABLE ACTIVITIES This heading comprises all expenditure on activities pursuing the charity's objects. It should include grants payable and the costs of supporting charitable activities and projects (e.g. salaries, office, communications and other costs identifiable as an integral part of the cost of carrying out those charitable activities or projects), as well as depreciation of fixed assets where used wholly or mainly for charitable activities. The charity should describe the main charitable activities and attribute expenditure to them to give an indication of the way resources are expended. This should, as far as possible, mirror the activities shown under the incoming resources categories. A note to the accounts will give further analysis of the expenditure.

GOVERNANCE COSTS These are the general running costs of the charity, rather than specific costs incurred through fundraising or charitable activity. They will normally include internal and external audit, legal advice for trustees and costs associated with constitutional and statutory requirements, such as the cost of trustee meetings and preparing statutory accounts. Included within this category are any costs associated with the strategic as opposed to day-to-day management of the charity's activities.

The costs of governance of the charity will include both direct costs incurred in organisational administration and complying with statutory requirements, and indirect costs, such as staff time and office costs. A fair share of support costs should therefore be apportioned to governance costs.

Support costs

Support costs do not constitute an activity in themselves, but instead allow other activities to be undertaken. They are the central administration and management costs, finance, bookkeeping, payroll, IT and other support services. A rational apportionment of support costs should be undertaken to attribute these costs to the activities they support. As well as charitable activities, this apportionment should include activities to generate funds and governance of the charity. The chosen method of apportionment should reflect reality and be applied consistently from year to year. Common methods used include the following:

- staff numbers
- staff time
- level of direct cost on the activity before apportioned support costs

■ floor area occupied by the activity.

The costs of activities presented in the SoFA will include the support costs attributed to them. Since support costs may be a significant area of expenditure for many charities, the level and types of costs need to be explained further in the notes to the accounts. The notes need to explain the main elements of support costs and how they have been apportioned. You can choose how you describe the apportionment – whether by percentages, the amounts apportioned or explanation of the method chosen.

As well as showing the expenditure under these headings on the face of the SoFA, you need to describe the expenditure in 'natural' headings in the notes to the accounts. These are the categories of rent, rates, salaries etc. that we are accustomed to in ordinary accounts. The notes should also show how the totals on the SoFA are constituted.

Fund accounting

One of the main differences between charity and commercial accounts is the format showing that all incoming and outgoing resources, assets and liabilities belong to a fund in the charity's accounts. It is necessary to track funds through the accounts, so that one knows the amounts received and expended, and balances on each type of fund. The different types of funds are:

Permanent endowment funds – donations that have been given to a charity to be held as capital with no power to convert the funds to income. These may be cash or other assets.

Expendable endowment funds – donations that have been given to a charity to be held as capital, where the trustees have a discretionary power to use the funds as income.

■ **Restricted funds** – funds subject to special trusts specified by the donor. This could be because of a public appeal for a specific purpose, grants or donations. It may also include land, buildings or other assets donated to a charity. The trustees will be in breach of trust if they use restricted income other than for the specified purpose. Usually interest or other investment income on a restricted fund will be added to the fund. In some cases the terms of the donation will state how investment income should be applied. The various restricted funds may be grouped together, but should be separately disclosed in the notes to the accounts if significant.

Unrestricted funds – funds available for the purposes of the charity, to be spent as the trustees see fit.

Designated funds – unrestricted funds that have been earmarked for a particular purpose by the trustees. The notes to the accounts should explain the purpose of designated funds.

General funds – unrestricted funds that have not been earmarked and may be used generally to further the charity's objects.

Other requirements of SORP

The SORP sets out how certain areas should be handled for the purposes of the SORP. These are looked at in detail in *A Practical Guide to Charity Accounting* (Directory of Social Change, 2003) and therefore only the most important are mentioned here, in checklist form:

Gifts in kind are assets donated to the charity, which should be included at their value to the charity both as a donation and an asset within the appropriate income category.

Donated services should be included if there is a cost to a third party in providing the service. Include under donations and the relevant expense heading at the value to the recipient charity.

Volunteer help should not normally be included unless it is a donated service. Usually it is adequate to explain how volunteers contribute to the work of the charity in the trustees' annual report. If the charity makes significant use of volunteers, further information should be provided, outlining the activities they help to provide, the contribution in terms of hours and an estimate of the financial value of their contribution.

Investments should be revalued to market value at each balance sheet date, with unrealised gains and losses shown in the SoFA under the appropriate fund heading.

All incoming resources received and receivable should be included in the SoFA, including legacies and new endowments.

Funds for the purchase of fixed assets are included as restricted income, with the related depreciation being charged to the fund, thus reducing it over the life of the related assets

Annual accounting requirements of charities in England and Wales

The annual accounting requirements of unincorporated charities are set out in Part VI of the Charities Act 1993, as updated by the Charities Act 2006, and the Accounts and Reports Regulations 1995 and 2005. Charitable companies follow company legislation (see below).

Charities must prepare accounts in the correct format for each financial year and submit them to the Charity Commission within 10 months of the end of the financial year. The basic requirements are that larger charities must prepare a statement of financial activities (SoFA) and a balance sheet. The accounting regulations also specify explanatory notes – which must accompany the accounts – and the categories in which items should be shown in the main statements. There are some exceptions from the requirements for smaller unincorporated charities.

Charities with income less than £250,000

These charities must prepare accounts on the accruals basis and they must comply with the requirements of the accounting regulations and follow the recommendations of the SORP. Accruals accounts must consist of a SoFA and balance sheet. The SORP recommends that charities describe expenditure by activity and give details of the breakdown into the normal expense-type headings in the notes to the accounts. However, under the accounting regulations, smaller charities may simplify the description of their expenditure in the SoFA. This means that they may use the normal expense-type headings they may have used in their old income and expenditure account, i.e. salaries, rent, rates, light, heat etc. This means that the SoFA for many smaller charities will not be very different from an income and expenditure account. It is likely that the limit will be raised to £500,000 for this relief when the accounting regulations are updated. The Charity Commission website will contain information about such changes as well as further guidance for these charities.

Charities with income £100,000 or less

Unincorporated charities with gross income of not more than £100,000 may choose to prepare a simpler form of accounts, comprising a receipts and payments account accompanied by a statement of assets and liabilities. This will be instead of the SoFA and balance sheet. There is no prescribed format set out in the regulations, but the Charity Commission have produced practical guidance with example accounts in guidance available from their website.

Charities with income less than £10,000

These charities have to prepare accounts, but do not have to submit them to the Charity Commission unless requested to do so. In the case of unincorporated charities, these may be on the receipts and payments basis.

Exempt charities

These are certain categories of charities, which are exempt from registration with the Charity Commission and the sections of the Act relating to accounts and audit. In practice these charitable bodies are usually already subject to specific provisions relating to their accounts and audit under other regulatory bodies. Exempt charities are listed in Schedule 2 to the Charities Act 1993. As a result of the Charities Act 2006 and ensuing regulations, many of these charities will be brought onto the charity register and will have to comply with these aspects of charity law.

The accounts of these charities should follow the SORP, unless a more specific SORP applies e.g. higher education or registered social landlords.

Excepted charities

These are certain categories of charities, which do not have to register with the Charity Commission, although they may register if they wish. If they do register, they must send in their annual report and accounts to the Charity Commission. However, if they are not registered, they do not need to submit reports and accounts. The trustees still have a statutory duty to prepare annual accounts and they have to comply with other requirements, such as sending their accounts to a member of the public if requested to do so.

Charitable companies

The relevant sections of the Charities Act 1993 (sections 41–44) and accounting regulations 3 to 9 concerning the form and content of accounts do not apply to charitable companies. They are required to prepare accounts in the form prescribed by the Companies Acts and these accounts must show a true and fair view. In order to comply with the requirement to show a true and fair view, charitable companies will be expected to comply with the SORP. In practice, therefore, the format of their accounts should be very similar to that of unincorporated charities, although certain charitable companies may need to prepare a summary income and expenditure account as well as a SoFA. It does mean that charitable companies cannot opt for the receipts and payments basis; all accounts of companies must be prepared on the accruals basis and must be submitted to Companies House within 10 months of the financial year end. Note that there are penalties for the late submission of accounts to Companies House, which start at £100 for accounts up to three months late and rise to £250 for accounts filed three to six months late, £500 for accounts filed six to twelve months late and £1,000 for accounts filed more than 12 months late. The time allowed to file accounts will be reduced to nine months as a result of the Companies Act 2006, with an implementation date scheduled for 2008.

Charity Commission filing

Apart from the small charities up to the £10,000 threshold, all registered charities, including charitable companies, must submit their annual report and accounts within 10 months of the financial year end to the Charity Commission. In addition, the Charity Commission asks charities to submit a completed annual return and a database update form. The information required on the annual return will include extracts from the accounts, so it may be easier to complete these at the same time.

Charity annual reports and accounts are available to download from the Charity Commission website.

In addition, members of the public may request a copy of the latest annual accounts of the charity and the charity must send them within two months. The charity may charge a reasonable fee for doing so, to cover photocopying and postage.

Charities with income greater than £1 million are also required to complete a Part C to the annual return, known as the Summary Information Return, or SIR. This asks for simple versions of information and financial highlights from the trustees' annual report and financial statements.

Audit requirements for charities in England and Wales

Since the enactment of the Charities Act 1993, unincorporated charities had been required by statute to have an audit if their income was greater than £250,000. The audit regime for companies is set out in the Companies Acts and the threshold for charitable companies was also set at £250,000.

New Charities and Companies Acts in 2006 introduced a raised threshold of £500,000 before an audit is required, together with an assets threshold of £2.4 million. The change takes effect for financial years commencing on or after 27 February 2007 – so will apply to year ends 28 February 2008 onwards.

The audit must be undertaken by a registered auditor – an auditor who is qualified to undertake audits of companies and is regulated in his or her work.

Independent examination for unincorporated charities

Charities below the audit threshold can choose to have an independent examination instead of an audit. For income at or below £250,000 the independent examination may be undertaken by anyone with some experience of accounting, but they do not have to be a qualified accountant or auditor. For independent examinations of larger charities, the examiner needs to be a qualified accountant (as defined on the Charity Commission website).

Charities in this category may choose to have an audit, if the trustees think it is wise or if they have relatively complex affairs. It will be necessary to have an audit if the constitution, or funders, requires it.

Very small charities (those with gross income and total expenditure not exceeding £10,000) do not need to have a statutory audit or an independent examination, but they also need to check their constitution and their funders' requirements.

Smaller and very small charities may need to contact the Charity Commission for advice on how their constitution may be amended so that they can take advantage of the reliefs from audit.

Audit of charitable companies

Larger charitable companies are required to have an audit by a registered auditor. Charitable companies with gross income below £250,000 and net assets of less than £1.4 million may opt to have an accountant's report instead of an audit. As described above, the audit threshold changes to £500,000 income or £2.4 million assets for companies for accounting periods beginning on or after 27 February 2007.

As various sections of the Companies Act 2006 are implemented in 2008, charitable companies will be under the same requirements as unincorporated charities and will be able to have an independent examination if their income is below the £500,000 threshold.

Companies with a gross income of up to £90,000 and a balance sheet total less than £1.4 million are not required to have an audit or an accountant's report unless their constitution or funders require it. All companies must prepare full accruals accounts and submit accounts to Companies House within 10 months of the end of the financial year (changing to nine months in 2008). In addition, 10 per cent of the membership can request that an audit be performed, even if the company otherwise qualifies for the exemption.

An accountant's report is independent confirmation that the accounts have been properly prepared from the accounting records. It does not seek to confirm that the accounting records themselves are complete and accurate. An accountant will often also prepare the accounts, although they could just review the accounts and compare them with the underlying records. The accountant ensures that the accounts are presented properly and disclose all the information required under the Companies Acts. He or she then reports under an 'Accountant's Report' confirming that the accounts have been properly prepared.

Accounting and audit requirements in England and Wales following implementation of Charities Act 2006 and Companies Act 2006

	Accounts	External scrutiny
Unincorporated charities		
Gross income over £500,000	Accruals basis following SORP	Audit by registered auditor
£250,000 – £500,000	Accruals basis following SORP	Independent examination by a qualified accountant

	Accounts	*External scrutiny*
£100,000 – £250,000	Accruals basis following SORP	Independent examination
£10,000 – £100,000	Receipts and payments account and statement of assets and liabilities	Independent examination
Less than £10,000	Receipts and Payments basis – no need to submit to Charity Commission	No external scrutiny required by statute

Charitable companies

Gross income over £500,000	Accruals basis following SORP	Audit by registered auditor
£90,000 – £500,000	Accruals basis following SORP	Accountant's report – changing to an independent examination in 2008
Less than £90,000	Accruals basis following SORP	No external scrutiny required

Trustees' annual report

As well as annual accounts, trustees of registered charities (and excepted charities if requested) must prepare an annual report, which has to be submitted to the Charity Commission together with the accounts. This requirement applies to charitable companies as well as unincorporated charities. However, companies may incorporate the information required under the Companies Acts for the directors' report into the trustees' annual report.

Very small charities with gross income or total expenditure not exceeding £10,000 do not have to prepare and file an annual report. Charities with income over £500,000 have to provide a fuller report. The detailed requirements are contained in the Charities (Accounts and Reports) Regulations 2005 and the SORP.

The trustees are jointly responsible for the annual report and it should therefore be approved at a normal trustees' meeting, following the procedure of the charity for such matters.

Structure of the trustees' annual report

Reference and administrative details

Structure, governance and management

Objectives and activities

Achievements and performance

Financial review

Plans for the future

Funds held as custodian trustee

Charities below the audit threshold are required to provide basic information about their activities. In each section below, the additional requirements for larger charities are also explained.

REFERENCE AND ADMINISTRATIVE DETAILS The reference and administrative details may be put onto one page before the narrative sections of the trustees' annual report. This section needs to include:

Name of the charity, the charity number, company number if registered and address of the principal office.

Trustees during the period of the report up to the date the report was approved.

Additional information required for charities above the audit threshold:

Senior staff to whom day-to-day management of the charity is delegated.

Names and addresses of advisers such as bankers, solicitors, auditors and investment managers.

STRUCTURE, GOVERNANCE AND MANAGEMENT This section should explain how the charity is constituted, its organisational structure and how the charity's decision-making processes operate. All charities should report:

The legal structure, e.g. trust, company limited by guarantee, unincorporated association.

How trustees are recruited and appointed.

Charities above the audit threshold additionally report:

The policies and procedures adopted for the induction and training of trustees.

The organisational structure of the charity and how decisions are made. For example, which types of decisions are taken by the charity trustees and which are delegated to staff.

Where the charity is part of a wider network (for example, charities affiliated within an umbrella group) the relationship involved should also be explained where this impacts on the operating policies adopted by the charity.

The relationships between the charity and related parties, including its subsidiaries, and with any other charities and organisations with which it co-operates.

A statement should be provided confirming that the major risks to which the charity is exposed, as identified by the trustees, have been reviewed and systems or procedures have been established to manage those risks. Note that larger charitable companies need to go further to comply with company legislation in this respect and provide more information on the major risks and uncertainties facing the charity.

OBJECTIVES AND ACTIVITIES The report should explain what the charity's objects are and what it does in order to achieve them. All charities have to state the objects of the charity as set out in its governing document.

Charities above the audit threshold additionally report:

The charity's aims and mission.

Main objectives for the year.

Strategies to achieve those objectives.

Details of significant activities, such as main programmes, projects and services provided, that contribute to the achievement of the objectives.

Grantmaking policies where this is a significant activity.

Information about the role and contribution of volunteers, such as the activities volunteers help to provide, their contribution in terms of hours or staff equivalents, and an indicative value of this contribution.

ACHIEVEMENTS AND PERFORMANCE All charities have to provide a summary of the main achievements of the charity during the year.

Charities above the audit threshold should provide a review of their performance against set objectives, giving both qualitative and quantitative information such as indicators, milestones and benchmarks against which the achievement is assessed. In particular, the report should contain:

A review of charitable activities undertaken to explain performance.

Comment on fundraising performance.

Details of the performance of investment compared with the policy.

Comment on those factors affecting performance.

FINANCIAL REVIEW The report should contain a review of the financial position of the charity and the main financial management policies adopted in the year, including:

The reserves policy, stating the level of reserves and why they are held. This should include designated funds and the likely timing of future expenditure from those funds.

If there are funds in deficit, the reasons for, and plans to eliminate, the deficit.

Charities above the audit threshold should additionally report:

Principal funding sources and how expenditure in the year under review has supported the key objectives of the charity.

The investment policy and objectives, including any social, environmental or ethical policies.

PLANS FOR THE FUTURE Only charities above the audit threshold need to provide information under this section. They need to describe the charity's plans for the future, including the aims and key objectives it has set for future periods together with details of any activities planned to achieve them.

FUNDS HELD AS CUSTODIAN TRUSTEE If a charity holds funds as a custodian trustee, then the following additional details are needed:

Description of the assets it holds in this capacity.

The name and objects of the charity (or charities) on whose behalf the assets are held and how this activity falls within its own objects.

Details of the arrangements for safe custody and segregation of such assets from the charity's own assets.

SUMMARY

Charity accounts have come under increasing scrutiny from regulators and the public, so compliance with the annual reporting regime is required. However, well presented annual accounts will also help charities to fundraise and promote their cause.

7 Interpreting accounts

INTRODUCTION

Accounts give us information about the past performance of an organisation and its overall financial health. We can therefore gather information about the organisation's viability and how well it is managed. Care is needed when interpreting financial accounts, however, as there is often too little information to come to a firm conclusion. Accounts will simply give us pointers towards the questions that need to be asked and the lines of inquiry to pursue.

Interpreting accounts requires a combination of a little technical knowledge and plenty of practice. Chapter 5 covers some of the basics of understanding accounts; the Glossary on page 197 explains much of the jargon. This chapter covers some of the more technical areas and gives you an opportunity to practise, using a case study included at the end of the chapter. More practice will help to develop your skill at asking the right questions.

READING ACCOUNTS

A full set of charity accounts will consist of:

☐ Trustees' report

☐ Statement of financial activities (SoFA)

☐ Balance sheet

☐ Notes to the accounts

■ Auditor's report or independent examiner's report

Larger or more complex charities may additionally produce

☐ Consolidated statement of financial activities

☐ Summary income and expenditure account

☐ Cashflow statement

Small charities taking advantage of exemptions may produce a simpler form of accounts, such as a receipts and payments account, summary of movements on the bank and cash balances and a statement of assets and liabilities. This form of accounts gives less information, but requires less interpretation and is therefore not covered in detail in this chapter. The Charity Commission publishes helpful guidance on accounts for smaller charities.

The first thing to establish is whether you have a full set of accounts. An incomplete set will not be helpful; in particular, the notes to the accounts will provide key information. You should also check that the trustees have approved the annual accounts by looking for their signature on the balance sheet. The audit report or independent examiner's report should also be signed and dated. These signatures indicate that you are looking at final approved and audited or examined accounts, not at draft accounts.

Trustees' annual report

The trustees' annual report is worth reading, both as an introduction to the accounts and for the commentary on activities and performance. A good report should highlight significant financial transactions during the year and explain the salient features of the accounts. It should also link the description of the aims and activities of the charity to the financial accounts.

Statement of financial activities and balance sheet

The main financial statements are the statement of financial activities (SoFA) and the balance sheet. The SoFA replaces the income and expenditure account (profit and loss account) for charities. However, note that where the charity has no endowment funds, the SoFA will be substantially the same as an income and expenditure account.

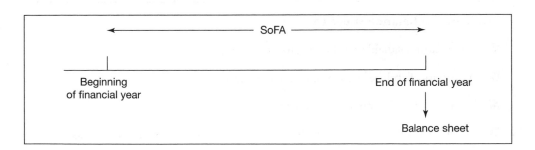

The SoFA looks back over the past, drawing together all the transactions for the period covered by the accounts, in this case a year. (It will usually be a year, unless the charity is new or changing its financial year end for some reason.) It shows the totals for resources becoming available to the charity and resources expended for that year.

The balance sheet is a snapshot of the position at the end of the financial year. (The date of the balance sheet should always coincide with the date to which the SoFA is made up.) The balance sheet indicates the level of reserves available to the charity, as well as the assets and liabilities which represent those reserves. The balance sheet straddles the end of one accounting year and the beginning of the next. It gives us important information about the financial health and viability of the organisation.

The SoFA and the balance sheet interlink (see the examples). The lower half of the balance sheet contains information about the balances on the various funds at the end of the financial year – this is the same information as at the bottom of the SoFA. This is not a coincidence, but a consequence of balancing your accounts properly. The SoFA explains the charity's transactions over the year and shows the net results. The results accumulate over time and lead to the balances in the funds of the balance sheet. These funds are represented by the assets and liabilities on the top half of the balance sheet. The total funds of a charity are always matched by the net assets.

Look in the SoFA for:

■ Total incoming resources and size of the charity

■ Types of incoming resources available to the charity

■ What the charity spends its money on

■ Amount spent on administration and fundraising

■ Unspent restricted and unrestricted funds for the year and balances carried forward

---

Look in the balance sheet for:

■ Total funds available to the charity (or reserves)

■ Assets and liabilities belonging to each fund

■ Liquidity and the charity's ability to meet its debts

■ Funds available to the charity for specific purposes as designated funds

■ Balances on restricted funds for future expenditure

Notes to the accounts

The notes to the accounts expand on particular lines in the SoFA and balance sheet, and you should refer to the notes as you read through the main financial statements. The number of notes will increase as a charity gets more complex. There will also be more information tucked away in the notes as it is not possible to include such details on the SoFA or balance sheet. It is therefore important to read *all* the notes.

The accounting policies are there to explain the methods used to make judgements about how to treat certain items. It is not possible for every organisation to adopt exactly the same approach. Although the SORP sets down certain treatments, there are several areas where the charity still has to state what the treatment is. It is good practice to explain the treatments even if these do conform to the SORP.

Example SoFA

The example SoFA shows incoming resources and resources expended by fund, with a separate column for each fund. The SoFA is a summary; more detailed workings deal with each specific fund. The column for endowment shows that £253,000 of new endowment funds were received in the year from donations and legacies. More detail about existing and new endowment funds would have to be given in the notes to the accounts. Further down the page, we see that the endowment fund also increased by £30,000 of unrealised gains. These arise because the endowment funds are invested (see 'investments' under 'fixed assets' on the balance sheet). At the end of the financial year, the investments must be revalued to the market value at the date of the balance sheet. The investments have increased in value, so there is a corresponding gain in the endowment fund. Because the investments have not been sold, the gain is called *unrealised*; realised gains or losses are made when investments are sold.

The charity receives restricted income from funders for its charitable childcare work. It also generates unrestricted income from its charitable activities through fees for parenting classes.

The net incoming resources are the result of subtracting total resources expended from total incoming resources. It is the rough equivalent to surplus or deficit, although this term is not appropriate in the SoFA since it includes more than income and expenditure. This example SoFA tells us that this charity spends nearly all its incoming resources in the year, the exception being the endowments. The funds brought forward show us the level of reserves from previous years. Since they are not high relative to overall income, this would seem to be the regular practice of this charity.

EXAMPLE STATEMENT OF FINANCIAL ACTIVITIES

	Endowment £'000	Restricted £'000	Unrestricted £'000	This year Total £'000	Last year Total £'000
Incoming resources					
Incoming resources from generated funds					
Voluntary income	253	27	15	295	57
Investment income	–	–	25	25	13
Incoming resources from charitable activities					
Childcare grants	–	257	50	307	295
Parenting classes	–	–	245	245	239
Total incoming resources	253	284	335	872	604
Resources expended					
Costs of generating funds					
Fundraising and publicity	–	–	21	21	29
Charitable activities					
Childcare work	–	279	51	330	316
Parenting classes	–	–	226	226	209
Governance costs	–	–	36	36	35
Total resources expended	0	279	334	613	589
Net incoming resources before transfers	253	5	1	259	15
Unrealised gains on investment assets	30	–	–	30	22
Net movement in funds	283	5	1	289	37
Reconciliation of funds					
Total funds brought forward	250	30	73	353	316
Total funds carried forward	533	35	74	642	353

Looking at the SoFA, one can see that this charity is heavily dependent on grants and fees for the main charitable activities. The small amount of income it can earn in investment income from the endowment fund is available for spending on the charitable purposes.

Example balance sheet

The stock, debtors, creditors and cash at bank are the components of the working capital of this charity. These elements move through the working capital cycle to fund the cashflow. This part of the balance sheet can be likened to a snapshot of the charity. The amounts shown under each category are only true for that particular day. The next day, the amount shown as due under debtors could arrive and be banked. This would change the snapshot, reducing debtors and increasing cash at bank. Note that the overall current assets would not change. If some of the creditors were paid, this would reduce the amounts due to creditors and for cash at bank. Again, note that this would not change the net current assets.

The amount of net current assets gives a good indication of the level of working capital available. Even though the exact amounts under each category are only true for that particular day, the net current assets figure will only change with significant new transactions and indicates the level of funds available to the charity. The net current assets provide proof that the charity can manage its cashflow and meet the debts shown under creditors. Where the current assets include significant amounts for debtors, it is better to calculate whether the cash at bank is sufficient to pay the creditors. Thus, we can see in the example balance sheet that there is £105,000 in the bank to pay current liabilities of £94,000.

Note: A charity that has net current liabilities is technically insolvent. It will need the support of a bank or other funders to pay the creditors. Whilst this is a difficult position to be in, a charity does not have to wind up. It must, however, take action to improve the position and will not be able to carry on indefinitely in a position of net current liabilities. An organisation is insolvent when it cannot pay its debts. It should stop all activity at that point, and obtain advice from an accountant or insolvency practitioner.

The example balance sheet shows that £213,000 is invested in fixed assets. The charity does not have this much in unrestricted funds. However, there is a creditor due after more than one year, of £135,000. This is a long-term loan and has probably been borrowed for a fixed asset, such as a building. It is therefore likely that this is a mortgage. In a full set of accounts you would look through the notes to the accounts, which should reveal the nature of the fixed assets and whether they had been given as security for the loan.

EXAMPLE BALANCE SHEET	This year		Last year	
	£'000	£'000	£'000	£'000
Fixed assets				
Tangible fixed assets		213		215
Investments		533		250
		746		465
Current assets				
Stock	5		4	
Debtors	15		17	
Cash at bank and in hand	105		89	
	125		110	
Current liabilities				
Creditors: amounts due within one year	94		70	
Net current assets		31		40
Total assets less current liabilities		777		505
Creditors: amounts due after more than one year		135		152
Net assets		642		353
Funds				
Endowment funds:				
Permanent endowment		533		250
Restricted income funds		35		30
Unrestricted income funds:				
Designated		28		28
General		46		45
Total charity funds		642		353

Note that the balance sheet value of the investments is equal to the value of the endowment fund. The charity has to keep the endowment fund intact and has probably invested it for the long term.

The overall picture is of a reasonably healthy, solvent charity. However, the reserves are low. General funds only represent 27 days of operating costs, so it would have difficulty continuing in the event of a drop in income.

CASE STUDY – INTERPRETING ACCOUNTS

Interpret the information given in the example charity accounts, which follow. Consider the following basic questions, but also add any information or comments. A suggested interpretation is given at the end of the chapter.

1. Does the Centre have more assets than liabilities?

2. Does it have money in the bank?

3. Who owes it money?

4. Who does it owe money to?

5. When will it have to pay off its liabilities?

6. Is it carrying forward funds to next year?

7. Where does most of its income come from?

8. Is it heavily dependent on one source of income?

9. What proportion of its income does it spend on staff costs?

10. What proportion of its income does it spend on raising funds and governance?

BORSETSHIRE DRUGS ADVICE CENTRE

Reference and administrative details

For the year ended 31 March 2007

Company number	1032145
Charity number	1234567
Registered office and operational address	10 High Street Borcester Borsetshire BA1 6PR

Trustees

Trustees, who are also directors under company law, who served during the year and up to the date of this report were as follows:

Mr P Archer	Chair
Mrs L Snell	Vice Chair
Miss U Gupta	Treasurer
Mrs M Antrobus	Secretary
Mr N Pargeter	
Mr J Woolley	
Mr G Pemberton (appointed 22 October 2006)	
Mrs J Aldridge (appointed 14 February 2007)	
Mrs S Hebden (resigned 24 September 2006)	
Mr T Forrest (resigned 11 November 2006)	

Principal staff

Mr J Black	Chief Executive
Mrs J Hoover	Deputy Chief Executive

Bankers

National Bank of England
13 Tie Street
Collingdon
N18 3JU

Solicitors

Braithewaite & Co.
15 Court Street
Collingdon
N18 3JU

Auditors

Biggs & Co
Chartered accountants and registered auditors
High Street
Borchester
BA1 8BR

BORSETSHIRE DRUGS ADVICE CENTRE

Report of the trustees

For the year ended 31 March 2007

The trustees present their report and the audited financial statements for the year ended 31 March 2007.

Reference and administrative information set out on page 1 forms part of this report. The financial statements comply with current statutory requirements, the memorandum and articles of association and the Statement of Recommended Practice – Accounting and Reporting by Charities (issued in March 2005).

Structure, governance and management

The organisation is a charitable company limited by guarantee, incorporated on 8 August 1992 and registered as a charity on 21 July 1990.

The company was established under a memorandum of association which established the objects and powers of the charitable company and is governed under its articles of association.

The trustees are appointed at the AGM each year and select a chair, vice chair, treasurer and secretary amongst themselves. The trustees meet at least six times a year and consider the strategy and policies of the charity. They are responsible for appointing the chief executive and deputy chief executive. The day-to-day management of the charity is delegated to the chief executive.

Objectives and activities

The charity is established to educate people in the area of Borsetshire about the effects of all drug use. The charity runs three activities in order to achieve this.

Advice and information

This project is based at the central office and provides help and advice to drug users, parents, teachers, social workers and others wanting to know more about the effects of drug use. Several information leaflets have been produced and these are now available in doctors' surgeries, Borsetshire Royal Infirmary and the citizens' advice bureaux in the area. Individual advice is provided at drop-in times and also by special appointment. As a result of the advice service, a parents' support group has been set up on the Borchester Green Estate.

The project is funded by the Borsetshire County Council and employs four members of staff. The mainstay of the service are the many volunteers who provide advice and distribute information leaflets. In the year under review over 1,000 volunteer hours were donated and 1,200 people were assisted. The receipt of a donation from the Berrow Estate Charitable Trust has enabled us to buy a new computer and database software, which will be used to organise information and make it more easily accessible.

Outreach

A team of four staff work from the central office and go out to meet young people who are either at risk of getting into drug use or already drug users. The team also gets the information out to young people on estates and into clubs to make them aware of the consequences of drug use.

Café

The contract with Borsetshire County Council to run a café in the centre of Borchester continues to run successfully. All the staff working in the café are former drug users training in catering. On average about 75 people use the café each day, which is an increase of 50 per cent compared with the attendance when it was run by the Social Services Department. The café still operates from the same premises owned by the County Council, which were given a complete facelift two years ago. Now the bright and cheerful atmosphere hosts all sorts of activities, including art exhibitions, jazz evenings and other theme evenings.

Reserves policy

The trustees have established a policy whereby the unrestricted funds not committed or invested in tangible fixed assets should be between three and six months of annual running costs, which equates to £60,000–£120,000 in general funds. This would enable the charity to continue its current activities in the event of a drop in income, while the trustees considered how to replace the funding or change the activities. At present the level of reserves is £23,196 and does not therefore reach the target level. The trustees are considering ways in which the target level can be attained.

Investment policy

Sufficient funds are retained in short-term deposit accounts at any one time to ensure that the charity can meet all its liabilities. Funds available for longer-term investment are few and therefore a specialised charity unit trust has been selected for all the remaining investment funds, as this provides the balance between income and capital growth the trustees require. The return on investments in the year at over 8 per cent is considered satisfactory.

Plans for future

The charity plans to continue the activities as outlined above, subject to satisfactory funding arrangements. In addition, the trustees plan to introduce a new scheme to place rehabilitated drug users who have been through our training projects on mentoring schemes with local employers.

Statement of responsibilities of the trustees

The trustees are required to prepare financial statements for each financial year, which give a true and fair view of the state of affairs of the charity and the incoming resources and application of resources, including the net income or expenditure, of the charity for the year. In preparing those financial statements the trustees are required to:

- select suitable accounting policies and then apply them consistently;
- make judgements and estimates that are reasonable and prudent;
- state whether applicable accounting standards and statements of recommended practice have been followed, subject to any material departures disclosed and explained in the financial statements; and
- prepare the financial statements on the going concern basis unless it is inappropriate to presume that the charity will continue in operation.

The trustees are responsible for keeping proper accounting records which disclose with reasonable accuracy at any time the financial position of the charity and enable them to ensure that the financial statements comply with the Companies Act 1985. The trustees are also responsible for safeguarding the assets of the charity and hence for taking reasonable steps for the prevention and detection of fraud and other irregularities.

The trustees confirm that, to the best of their knowledge, there is no information relevant to the audit of which the auditors are unaware. The trustees also confirm that they have taken all necessary steps to ensure that they themselves are aware of all relevant audit information and that this information has been communicated to the auditors.

Members of the charity guarantee to contribute an amount not exceeding £1 to the assets of the charity in the event of its winding up. The total number of such guarantees at 31 March 2007 was 8 (2006–8). The trustees are members of the charity but this entitles them only to voting rights. The trustees have no beneficial interest in the charity.

Auditors

Biggs & Co were re-appointed as the charitable company's auditors during the year and have expressed their willingness to continue in that capacity.

Approved by the trustees on 8 July 2007 and signed on their behalf by

Miss U Gupta – Treasurer   Mr P Archer – Chair

BORSETSHIRE DRUGS ADVICE CENTRE

Statement of financial activities (incorporating an income and expenditure account) For the year ended 31 March 2007

	Note	Restricted £	Unrestricted £	2007 Total £	2006 Total £
Incoming resources					
Incoming resources from generated funds					
Voluntary income	2	5,000	–	**5,000**	6,796
Investment income		765	900	**1,665**	1,324
Incoming resources from charitable activities					
Advice and information		70,000	–	**70,000**	60,000
Outreach work		80,000	–	**80,000**	66,132
Café income		–	115,000	**115,000**	98,414
Total incoming resources		155,765	115,900	**271,665**	232,666
Resources expended	3				
Costs of generating funds:					
Costs of generating voluntary income		–	2,179	**2,179**	1,893
Charitable activities					
Advice and information		68,917	–	**68,917**	61,756
Outreach work		68,829	–	**68,829**	53,316
Café		–	96,500	**96,500**	67,606
Governance costs		1,250	8,114	**9,364**	7,372
Total resources expended		138,996	106,793	**245,789**	191,943
Net incoming resources before transfers	4	16,769	9,107	**25,876**	40,723
Gross transfers between funds		438	(438)	**–**	–
Net income for the year		17,207	8,669	**25,876**	40,723
Unrealised gains on investment assets		–	762	**762**	202
Net movement in funds		17,207	9,431	**26,638**	40,925
Reconciliation of funds					
Total funds brought forward		1,316	25,594	**26,910**	(14,015)
Total funds carried forward	6	18,523	35,025	**53,548**	26,910

Borsetshire Drugs Advice Centre

Balance sheet

As at 31 March 2007

	Note	£	**2007** **£**	2006 £
Fixed assets				
Tangible fixed assets	7		**11,250**	10,000
Investments	8		**11,654**	10,892
			22,904	20,892
Current assets				
Debtors	9	**7,835**		5,628
Cash at bank and in hand		**31,193**		9,142
		39,028		14,770
Liabilities				
Creditors: amounts due within one year	10	**8,384**		8,752
Net current assets			**30,644**	6,018
Net assets	11		**53,548**	26,910
Funds	12			
Restricted income funds			**18,523**	1,316
Unrestricted income funds				
Designated funds			**10,000**	–
General funds			**23,196**	24,527
Revaluation fund			**1,829**	1,067
Total charity funds			**53,548**	26,910

Approved by the trustees on 8 July 2007 and signed on their behalf by

Miss U Gupta – Treasurer   Mr P Archer – Chair

INDEPENDENT AUDITORS' REPORT

To the members of

Borsetshire Drugs Advice Centre

We have audited the financial statements of Borsetshire Drugs Advice Centre for the year ended 31 March 2007 which comprise the statement of financial activities, balance sheet and related notes. These financial statements have been prepared in accordance with the accounting policies set out therein and the requirements of Statement of Recommended Practice: Accounting and Reporting by Charities (issued in March 2005).

This report is made solely to the charitable company's members, as a body, in accordance with section 235 of the Companies Act 1985. Our audit work has been undertaken so that we might state to the charitable company's members those matters we are required to state to them in an auditors' report and for no other purpose. To the fullest extent permitted by law, we do not accept or assume responsibility to anyone other than the charitable company and the charitable company's members, as a body, for our audit work, for this report, or for the opinions we have formed.

Respective responsibilities of the trustees and auditors

The trustees, who are also directors of Borsetshire Drugs Advice Centre for the purposes of company law, are responsible for preparing the annual report and the financial statements in accordance with applicable law, United Kingdom Accounting Standards (United Kingdom Generally Accepted Accounting Practice) and the Statement of Recommended Practice: Accounting and Reporting by Charities (issued in March 2005). The responsibilities of the trustees are set out in the statement of responsibilities of the trustees.

Our responsibility is to audit the financial statements in accordance with relevant legal and regulatory requirements and International Standards on Auditing (UK and Ireland).

We report to you our opinion as to whether the financial statements give a true and fair view and are properly prepared in accordance with the Companies Act 1985. We report to you whether, in our opinion, the information given in the annual report of the trustees is consistent with the financial statements. We also report to you if the charitable company has not kept proper accounting records, if we have not received all the information and explanations we require for our audit, or if information specified by law regarding the trustees' remuneration and other transactions is not disclosed.

We read other information contained in the annual report, and consider whether it is consistent with the audited financial statements. This other information comprises only the report of the trustees. We consider the implications for our report if we become aware of any apparent misstatements or material inconsistencies with the financial statements. Our responsibilities do not extend to any other information.

Basis of opinion

We conducted our audit in accordance with International Standards on Auditing (UK and Ireland) issued by the Auditing Practices Board. An audit includes examination, on a test basis, of evidence relevant to the amounts and disclosures in the financial statements. It also includes an assessment of the significant estimates and judgements made by the trustees in the preparation of the financial statements, and of whether the accounting policies are appropriate to the charitable company's circumstances, consistently applied and adequately disclosed.

We planned and performed our audit so as to obtain all the information and explanations which we considered necessary in order to provide us with sufficient evidence to give reasonable assurance that the financial statements are free from material misstatement, whether caused by fraud or other irregularity or error. In forming our opinion we also evaluated the overall adequacy of the presentation of information in the financial statements.

Opinion

In our opinion:

- the financial statements give a true and fair view, in accordance with United Kingdom Generally Accepted Accounting Practice as modified by the Statement of Recommended Practice: Accounting and Reporting by Charities (issued in March 2005), of the charitable company's state of affairs as at 31 March 2007 and of its incoming resources and application of resources, including its income and expenditure, for the year then ended; and
- the financial statements have been properly prepared in accordance with the Companies Act 1985; and
- the information given in the report of the trustees is consistent with the financial statements.

Biggs & Co
Chartered accountants & registered auditors
Borchester

BORSETSHIRE DRUGS ADVICE CENTRE

Notes to the financial statements

For the year ended 31 March 2007

1. Accounting policies

a) The financial statements have been prepared under the historical cost convention and in accordance with applicable accounting standards and the Companies Act 1985. They follow the recommendations in the Statement of Recommended Practice, Accounting and Reporting by Charities (issued in March 2005).

b) Voluntary income is received by way of donations and gifts and is included in full in the statement of financial activities when receivable.

c) Revenue grants are credited to the statement of financial activities when received or receivable whichever is earlier.

Where unconditional entitlement to grants receivable is dependent upon fulfilment of conditions within the charity's control, the incoming resources are recognised when there is sufficient evidence that conditions will be met. Where there is uncertainty as to whether the charity can meet such conditions, the incoming resource is deferred.

d) Restricted funds are to be used for specific purposes as laid down by the donor. Expenditure which meets these criteria is charged to the fund.

e) Unrestricted funds are donations and other incoming resources received or generated for the charitable purposes.

f) Designated funds are unrestricted funds earmarked by the trustees for particular purposes.

g) Costs of generating funds relate to the costs incurred by the charitable company in inducing third parties to make voluntary contributions to it, as well as the cost of any activities with a fundraising purpose.

Where information about the aims, objectives and projects of the charity is provided to potential beneficiaries, the costs associated with this publicity are allocated to charitable expenditure.

Where such information about the aims, objectives and projects of the charity is also provided to potential donors, activity costs are apportioned between fundraising and charitable activities on the basis of the area of literature occupied by each activity.

h) Resources expended are recognised in the period in which they are incurred. Resources expended include attributable VAT which cannot be recovered.

Resources expended are allocated to the particular activity where the cost relates directly to that activity. However, the cost of overall direction and administration of each activity, comprising the salary and overhead costs of the central function, is apportioned on the following basis which is an estimate, based on staff time, of the amount attributable to each activity.

Advice and information	20%
Outreach work	20%
Café	30%
Fundraising and publicity	10%
Governance costs	10%
Support costs	10%

Support costs are re-allocated to each of the activities on the following basis, which is an estimate, based on staff numbers, of the amount attributable to each activity:

Advice and information	26%
Outreach work	26%
Café	40%
Governance	8%

Governance costs are the costs associated with the governance arrangements of the charity. These costs are associated with constitutional and statutory requirements and include any costs associated with the strategic management of the charity's activities.

k) Depreciation is provided at rates calculated to write down the cost of each asset to its estimated residual value over its expected useful life, which in each case is set at four years.

Items of equipment are capitalised where the purchase price exceeds £500. Depreciation costs are allocated to activities on the basis of the use of the related assets in those activities. Assets are reviewed for impairment if circumstances indicate their carrying value may exceed their net realisable value and value in use.

m) Stocks are stated at the lower of cost and net realisable value. In general, cost is determined on a first in first out basis and includes transport and handling costs. Net realisable value is the price at which stocks can be sold in the normal course of business after allowing for the costs of realisation. Provision is made where necessary for obsolete, slow moving and defective stocks.

2. Voluntary income

	Restricted £	Unrestricted £	2007 Total £	2006 Total £
Donations:				
Berrow Estate Charitable Trust – for the purchase of computer equipment	5,000	–	5,000	–
For the general purposes of the charity	–	–	–	6,796
Total	5,000	–	5,000	6,796

BORSETSHIRE DRUGS ADVICE CENTRE

Notes to the financial statements

For the year ended 31 March 2007

3. Total resources expended

	Costs of generating funds £	Outreach work £	Café £	Advice and information £	Governance costs £	Support costs £	2007 £	2006 £
Staff costs (Note 5)	1,252	60,568	82,766	64,239	1,252	1,252	211,329	159,611
Recruitment	–	1,426	1,212	–	–	–	2,638	2,817
Travel	–	482	396	324	166	–	1,368	956
Premises	–	3,931	5,084	1,646	–	–	10,661	10,562
Communications	393	588	1,144	594	393	393	3,505	3,816
Legal and professional	–	–	–	–	1,250	–	1,250	2,429
Audit and accountancy	–	–	–	–	2,000	–	2,000	2,800
Consultancy	–	770	2,562	–	2,336	–	5,668	2,825
Volunteer expenses	95	–	1,428	1,489	–	–	3,012	2,791
Depreciation	–	625	1,250	625	1,250	–	3,750	2,500
Bank charges	–	–	–	–	608	–	608	836
Total resources expended	1,740	68,390	95,842	68,917	9,255	1,645	245,789	191,943
Support costs	439	439	658	–	109	(1,645)	–	–
Total resources expended	2,179	68,829	96,500	68,917	9,364	–	245,789	383,886

BORSETSHIRE DRUGS ADVICE CENTRE

Notes to the financial statements

For the year ended 31 March 2007

4. Net incoming resources for the year

	2007 £	2006 £
This is stated after charging:		
Depreciation	3,750	5,000
Auditors' remuneration:		
• audit	2,000	2,000
Trustees' remuneration	–	–
Trustees' reimbursed expenses	1,368	956

Trustees' reimbursed expenses represents the reimbursement of travel and subsistence costs of £1,368 (2006: £956) to members relating to attendance at meetings of the trustees.

5. Staff costs and numbers

	2007 £	2006 £
Staff costs were as follows:		
Salaries and wages	191,769	144,247
Social security costs	19,560	15,364
Pension contributions	–	–
	211,329	159,611
Total emoluments paid to staff were:	191,769	144,247

No employee earned more than £60,000 during the year.

The average weekly number of employees (full-time equivalent) during the year was as follows:

	2007 No.	2006 No.
Advice and Information	4.0	3.0
Outreach work	4.0	4.0
Café	6.0	6.0
Support costs	1.0	1.0
Governance costs	1.0	1.0
	16.0	15.0

6. Taxation

The charitable company is exempt from corporation tax as all its income is charitable and is applied for charitable purposes.

7. Tangible fixed assets

	Office equipment £	Total £
Cost		
At the start of the year	15,000	**15,000**
Additions in year	5,000	**5,000**
Disposals in year	–	–
At the end of the year	20,000	**20,000**
Depreciation		
At the start of the year	5,000	**5,000**
Charge for the year	3,750	**3,750**
Disposals in year	–	–
At the end of the year	8,750	**8,750**
Net book value at the end of the year	**11,250**	**11,250**
At the start of the year	10,000	**10,000**

8. Investments

	2007 £	2006 £
Market value at the start of the year	**10,892**	10,692
Unrealised gain/(loss)	**762**	202
Market value at the end of the year	**11,654**	10,894
Historic cost at the end of the year	**9,825**	9,825

9. Debtors

	2007 £	2006 £
Sundry debtors	**1,126**	1,048
Accrued income due on contracts	**6,709**	4,580
	7,835	5,628

10. Creditors: amounts due within one year

	2007 £	2006 £
Taxation and social security	**4,458**	3,896
Other creditors	**3,926**	4,856
	8,384	8,752

11. Analysis of net assets between funds

	Restricted funds £	Unrestricted funds £	Total funds £
Tangible fixed assets	3,750	7,500	**11,250**
Investments		11,654	**11,654**
Current assets	17,229	21,799	**39,028**
Creditors: amounts falling due within one year	(2,456)	(5,928)	**(8,384)**
Net assets at the end of the year	**18,523**	**35,025**	**53,548**
Unrealised gains included above on investments	–	1,829	**1,829**

12. Movements in funds

	At the start of the year £	Incoming resources £	Outgoing resources £	Unrealised gains on investments £	At the end of the year £
Restricted funds:					
a) Computer equipment	–	5,000	(1,250)	–	**3,750**
b) Advice and information	1,316	70,000	(68,917)	–	**2,399**
c) Outreach	–	80,765	(68,391)	–	**12,374**
Total restricted funds	1,316	155,765	(138,558)	–	**18,523**
Unrestricted funds:					
Designated funds:					
Purchase of new equipment	10,000	–	–	–	**10,000**
Total designated funds	10,000	–	–	–	**10,000**
General funds	15,594	115,900	(107,231)	762	**25,025**
Total unrestricted funds	25,594	115,900	(107,231)	762	**35,025**
Total funds	**26,910**	**271,665**	**(245,789)**	**762**	**53,548**

Purposes of restricted funds

The balances will be carried forward and used as follows:

a) The balance will fund future depreciation charges.
b) The balance will be used to continue the advice and information activity within the terms of the fund.
c) The balance arose from a delay in appointing new staff and will all be utilised in the forthcoming months.

Purposes of designated funds

The trustees have designated funds for purchase of new equipment in the café.

115

CASE STUDY – SUGGESTED INTERPRETATION

1. The Centre does have more assets than liabilities. This is shown by the net assets figure of £53,548 on the balance sheet, which is the same as the total funds. The assets that are actually available to the trustees to spend are the net current assets of £30,644, and they could sell the investments of £11,654 if necessary. However, some of these assets are part of the restricted funds, so they have to spend them in accordance with the terms of that funding. The trustees' report and note 12 to the accounts tell us that the majority of the restricted funds relate to the Outreach project, which has suffered from a shortage of staff. Whilst there seem to be quite a lot of assets on the balance sheet, not very much relates to 'free' reserves.

2. Yes, it does have money in the bank. This is found on the balance sheet; at the end of the year there was £31,193 in the bank. This was more than was needed at the time to meet the creditors of £8,384. This shows that the Centre is managing its cash quite well. Note that this is an improvement on the previous year, when it only had £9,142 to meet creditors of £8,752.

3. The debtors on the balance sheet are the people who owe the charity money. These are further explained in note 9 to the accounts. This shows that the local authority owes the majority of the debtors' figure, on the contract fees for the café training project.

4. It owes money to creditors in the balance sheet of £8,384, which is further explained in note 10 to the accounts. Approximately half the creditors' amount relates to outstanding tax and national insurance. The other half relates to other creditors and accruals, probably suppliers of goods and services.

5. All the liabilities are short-term; that is, they are creditors due within one year (current liabilities).

6. It is carrying forward funds to the next year. This is shown in the lower half of the balance sheet and also on the last line of the SoFA. The balance sheet shows a little more detail, as this breaks down the unrestricted funds into their components. We can see there that there are general funds of £23,196, which will have arisen from the surpluses over a number of years. There is also a revaluation fund of £1,829, which arises from revaluing the investments to market value. This is a surplus, but it has not yet been *realised*, i.e. the investments will have to be sold actually to achieve that profit or realise it. There are also designated funds, which are part of the charity's unrestricted funds. Note 12 to the accounts tells us that these have been designated for the purchase of new equipment for the café. This is similar to a charity saving up for items it plans to buy or projects it wishes to

fund. The charity is not obliged to spend the funds on that particular purpose; legally it must spend the funds to further its charitable objects, but there is no further restriction. The trustees could decide later that there is a higher priority for something else and re-designate the funds.

7. It receives most of its income from statutory grants and contracts from local government. These are for the three main areas of work: £70,000 for advice and information, £80,000 for outreach work and £95,000 for the café training project. The charity also earns some income from the café.

8. It is dependent on statutory sources for most of its income, even though this comes in three different tranches. It might be able to increase the earned income from the café, but this would not be significant.

9. It spends a very high proportion of it income on staff costs. Staff costs are £211,329 out of income of £271,665, which is nearly 78 per cent.

10. It spends a tiny proportion of its income on raising funds: just £2,179 or 0.8 per cent. It spends a little more on the governance of the charity: £9,364 or 3.4 per cent.

General comment

This is a fairly small charity running services with statutory funding. It is vulnerable to changes in the political climate or economic changes affecting local government funding and this would directly affect staffing levels and services. Most of its activity is concentrated on the services it provides and apparently spends little time or money on fundraising or general administration. It has a few fixed assets, but doesn't own property. It has a small 'buffer' in terms of some general funds, which are held partly as investment in unit trusts and partly in cash.

8 Computerisation

INTRODUCTION

People who do not like writing up their accounting records often think that a computer will be the answer. However, experience suggests that computerisation should be the second or third action on your list. It is wiser to set up a good manual system first and then consider computerised options. Computers can certainly assist in the financial management of an organisation, but you can also spend a great deal of time on setting them up and learning how to use them. Proper use of computers should be carefully planned and should be part of an organisation-wide information technology strategy.

This chapter does not attempt to be a specialist guide on the whole strategy an organisation should adopt for the use of computers. It does attempt to clarify some points on the use of computers in financial management and think through the decisions your own organisation may face. A book cannot tell you which computer software package to buy, and this chapter does not attempt to be a purchaser's guide. You need to make an assessment of your needs first and then look at the available options. New products are being launched all the time and you may need advice from someone who is independent and knowledgeable about the market.

SOFTWARE

Software consists of the programs that run on a computer; the computer itself is hardware. The most important decisions you will make are those about the type of software you need and this should be considered first. The hardware decision will follow logically, as you will know the type of equipment needed after you have assessed your software needs. Software can be designed for the needs of your particular organisation (bespoke software), but this is usually beyond the budget (or needs) of most smaller organisations. It also carries far more risk, and software packages may be purchased off the shelf for most tasks. The main types of software we are interested in for most office and finance functions are:

- wordprocessing

- database

- spreadsheet

- accounting package

- payroll package.

Wordprocessing

Writing letters and reports will often be the major use of computers in an office. You may wish to consider using wordprocessing software that will allow you to integrate figures from another package for a finance report. You will also be able to use a word-processing package to send out a standard letter to members or donors by using the mail merge function.

Many wordprocessing packages also allow you to do a certain amount of design and so they can be used for producing newsletters and publications. However, if you were serious about designing written material, you would probably use a desktop publishing package.

Things to consider when buying an off-the-shelf package:

- Will it do the job?

- Will it integrate into other systems?

- Can we get software maintenance and support and what will it cost?

- Do we have enough space on our computer(s)?

- Can we add 'bolt-on' software for our own specialist use?

Database

Membership charities and charities undertaking a large amount of fundraising from individuals will usually already have database packages for holding this information. You can buy a basic package, which is like an empty card index system – you buy the box and the cards and then set the system up. You can design the layout of the cards and reports, which will access and sort the information held on the database. You need to put careful thought into how you will want to use the information held in a database. It will probably take some time to input all the information, but once set up, it can become one of the most powerful and valuable parts of your organisation. You will be able to use it to send letters direct from the system or in conjunction with a wordprocessing package.

A database of members will usually contain details of when members paid their subscription. It therefore includes financial information and may form part of the accounting records. It is wise to try and set up systems in such a way that this information does not have to be duplicated for the financial records. There may be difficulties if the financial year and the subscription year are different, or in other ways if a clear cut-off is not operated on the membership database. A membership database that only records that the subscription was paid, with no further details, would be insufficient as a financial record. The subscription amount and date of receipt is needed, and probably also the date banked and a reference such as the paying in slip number or bank statement number if paid direct into the bank account. The membership database could then be used to produce a detailed list of membership receipts, so you wouldn't need to record the same level of detail in the cash book. The database will also be useful to the auditors when testing membership income.

In a similar way, a database of donors may be set up to keep records of requests for funding and responses. Again this can be done in such a way that the record of receipts provides further detail beyond the cash book. It will also be useful to the auditors when testing income.

Organisations providing services may wish to use a database as a log of service users and as a mailing list. The database could also be set up to produce invoices if you charge for goods or services. Entering the date of payment and the amount received would mean that the database could also be a sales ledger. This information would need to be duplicated in the main accounts, although only the totals would need to be input.

These suggestions are just examples of how you might explore the best use of systems and computer options. A database can be a part of the wider accounting records.

Fundraising packages

It is possible to buy specialist database packages that handle all the record keeping for managing a fundraising department. Many will be designed specifically to manage gift aid administration and will include the cards and reports for you to deal with gift aid donations (see Chapter 11). This cuts down the amount of time-consuming admin-istration normally associated with tax recovery on gift aid. However, you need to check that the system has been set up in the way you need it. For example, you may have donors who give by monthly standing order. If the system is only geared up to handle annual donations, it will not be suitable for your organisation. You may also want a package that can handle other donations, such as payroll giving, so also check this.

Some packages come with integrated accounting software, so you need to appraise this part of the software in case it is not suitable for your organisation.

Spreadsheet

Spreadsheet packages are a computerised form of a large sheet of paper containing a grid format. The great advantage with a spreadsheet is that it can perform calculations for you. It is also very easy to learn and start using a spreadsheet package. It is ideal for:

- budget preparation

- budget reports (e.g. comparing budget with actual)

- cashflow forecasts

- designing some forms

- summarising figures from main cash books

- writing financial reports (sections with calculations).

A spreadsheet allows you to make amendments and will automatically recalculate the totals. Thus you can set up a cashflow forecast at the beginning of the year, for example, and amend it as you obtain better information. You can enter the actual figures as these become known or you can delete the months that have passed and add on new months at the end.

Some people use spreadsheets for writing up cash books instead of having a manual cash book. This is an option, but you should consider the following points:

- it is easy to delete figures by mistake

- it is easy to put figures in the wrong column or row

- it is easy to assume that a formula is still correctly set up when in fact it is wrong because you have changed something else

- a mistake in setting it up will make the whole thing wrong

- it can be difficult for other people to access

- if the spreadsheet is large it can be difficult to read when you print it out (you may have to glue pieces of paper together and it is still difficult to scan across it all)

- you need to ensure that cross checks are built in to ensure that your spreadsheet adds across as well as down.

So you need to set the spreadsheet up carefully and check it manually with a calculator. In general, it is just as easy to keep a manual cash book if the number of transactions is small. If the number of transactions is large or growing, then consider using an appropriate accounting software package, which will be a better investment of your time in the long run.

Sophisticated users of spreadsheet packages will develop many more uses; and with a little time invested you could soon be producing colour graphs for your reports. Spreadsheet packages are useful for work with statistics as well as accounts and can also sort information.

Accounting package

An accounting package is a complete system for the organisation's bookkeeping. All such packages are based on the double entry bookkeeping system and so emulate a full manual bookkeeping system. You will find it easier to use most packages if you have a sound understanding of double entry bookkeeping and the meaning of terms such as debit and credit. It may therefore be wise to go on a training course to learn double entry bookkeeping and basic accounting before you attempt to computerise your accounts using an accounting software package. Trying to learn both the accounts and the computer aspects of a new system is quite daunting. You will also need to make decisions about how you want the system to be set up before you can begin using your accounting software. These decisions will be difficult unless you have a clear idea of what you want out of the system and can picture how it will work.

Accounting software packages will contain the various elements of the full book-keeping system. The nominal ledger is the central pillar of the whole system and every system will have this. The sales and purchase ledgers are often optional extras, as are management tools such as a stock control file and invoicing system.

Software varies as to whether exact equivalents of the cash book, sales day book, purchase day book and petty cash book are part of the system. Sometimes they are present as an inherent part of the system, but you do not see them as such. You will usually be able to print out reports to show the receipts, payments, purchases or sales for a particular period. You may wish to keep these reports in a folder to create your own daybook.

Once all the information has been entered, the totals on the nominal ledger accounts can be printed out in a list, known as a trial balance. This shows the amount on each account and whether the amount is a debit or a credit balance. This is the starting point for the preparation of accounts. The next step is to check certain key accounts and look into any balances that seem unusual. On most systems you will then be able to make adjusting entries, usually called journal entries. You will usually be able to produce a profit and loss account and balance sheet as the next stage.

On some systems, you will be able to change the profit and loss account to an income and expenditure account. Few systems can produce a statement of financial activities, but you should be able to get the information from the system and transfer it to the correct format. Most systems will produce accounts, but the amount of flexibility will vary from package to package.

There are very few specialist charity systems; most accounting software has been written with the commercial trader in mind. This will be fine for charities' trading subsidiaries, and many elements of a commercial system will apply to many charities. Every organisation needs a nominal ledger; many will need a purchase ledger. Charities selling goods or services will often need a sales ledger. These will all be the same, whatever your constitution is. This means that you should not be put off by the fact that a package has been written for a commercial user. What you should look for is flexibility – a system that allows you the freedom to use the parts that you need and ignore the parts that you don't need. Some packages are designed as modules, so you only buy the relevant modules; for example, you only buy the sales ledger module if you want to run a sales ledger.

Payroll package

Most payroll packages are very similar and so the choice should not be too difficult. Preparation of the payroll is a standardised task and all packages will follow HM Revenue & Customs (HMRC) rules and produce the records and forms required. The package should include an automatic update service for changes to the tax rates, personal allowances and so on. Check whether there is an extra charge for this service. You also need to check that the software company is well established and so able to fulfil its commitments. You would have to abandon a package that was no longer supported or updated. Many payroll packages are a module that can link into an accounting package. An integrated approach can be useful as it means that the transfers to the nominal ledger are undertaken automatically rather than manually.

You should consider the following when choosing a payroll package:

■ If we have weekly paid staff, can the package process weekly as well as monthly salaries?

■ Does the package produce all the end of year returns required by HMRC?

■ Is there a facility for the preparation of form P11D (Return of Expenses and Benefits)?

■ Can the system cope with submitting information electronically?

■ Can staff costs be analysed into cost centres?

■ Can the system deal with overtime, other additional payments, or varying hours?

■ Does the system include Statutory Sick Pay and Statutory Maternity Pay?

■ Can other deductions be made from net pay, such as union dues or loan repayments?

■ Does the system cope with pension contributions (if you have them), or payroll giving?

WHEN TO COMPUTERISE ACCOUNTS

When should an organisation buy an accounting software package and transfer all its bookkeeping and accounting onto it? The main advantage of computerising your accounts is that it should save time overall. It will take time to set up and learn the system, and to enter the data. Therefore the organisation should have a high enough volume of transactions to make the setting up worthwhile. Computers are good at handling a large volume of similar transactions. If your organisation has only about 20 transactions a month, then it is likely that the bookkeeping and accounting for the whole year could be done manually in the time it would take to set up a computerised package. However, you may wish to consider computerising when the volume of transactions is low if the organisation is growing. It is certainly going to be easier to learn the system and sort out teething problems whilst the organisation is small. You will need to be careful to choose a system that will be big enough for the organisation in the long run.

Charities differ from trading organisations in that the gross income or turnover might be quite small and yet the bookkeeping and accounting needs quite complex. This arises from the need for fund accounting under the SORP, the requirements of funders and the variety of sources of income and number of projects a charity may have. A trader may have just one source of income – sales of goods or services – and a straight-forward list of expenditure items. Charities will usually be more complex. In addition, their activities will often vary from year to year as new projects or activities are brought in and old ones are discontinued. The complexity of charity accounting may mean that a computerised system will save the organisation a lot of time.

Someone needs to be able to set up and operate the new accounting software, once it has been purchased. You must allow for the cost of staff training if you do not have someone who is already competent in the system. Computerising the accounts will be a big step for most organisations and if the people in the organisation are not happy or ready for it, it will fail. It will be more difficult for people just to look up when an invoice was paid (at first, anyway) and there may be resistance to learning about the new system.

Advantages of computerised accounts

Standardised format

Quick to enter data

Manual calculations eliminated

System will only allow balancing entries

Reports produced from system

Disadvantages of a computerised system

Less accessible for non-financial people in organisation

Personnel using the system need training

Untrained personnel may make mistakes which are difficult and costly to resolve

Poorly referenced systems may make the audit more difficult

Cheap or inappropriate packages may not incorporate sufficient controls

The process of computerising accounting records has several stages:

Assessing the organisation's needs

Preparing a specification

Choosing a package

Implementation plan

Testing

System operational

Assessing the organisation's needs

Before you buy your software package, you need to consider the organisation's needs in terms of accounting. A focus area for such an assessment should be the recording and reporting requirements of everyone in the organisation. It is essential to understand what you need to get out of the system as well as what you will be putting in. You will also need to gauge the size of the system required, access requirements and number of transactions. If possible, you should also try to think ahead to how the organisation may expand or what additional information may be needed in the future.

Illustration – Charity Training Services

Charity Training Services (CTS) runs short training courses in many subjects for the voluntary and public sectors. Fees are charged for the courses and most are led by freelance trainers. CTS has a small administrative staff and premises where the courses are run.

A review of CTS' needs reveals:

- it needs a system to log course bookings

- it needs to invoice people for course fees

- some people pay after they receive the invoice; others send payment with booking

- many customers book several courses at once for different individuals to attend training

- it has about 50 trainers, each leading about one session per week, submitting invoices weekly

- it only has five full-time staff

- it needs a weekly report that shows the number of course bookings received and can provide details of how many are booked onto each course

- it needs a monthly report to show income and expenditure compared with budget.

The organisation decides to buy a database program that can be tailored to its needs for course management. This will be a database of customers and will also be used to produce invoices and record whether payment has been received. It will also operate as the organisation's sales ledger and will be tied into the cash book receipts. CTS wants an accounting software package that allows it to bypass the sales ledger and input receipts direct onto the nominal ledger via a cash book routine. The database will also produce the weekly reports on bookings. It will also need to provide the basic information to identify how much course income has been invoiced in advance, so that the monthly income figures will correctly reflect the income earned on courses that ran in the month.

The accounting software needs to be a simple nominal ledger system with an integrated purchase ledger. This will allow CTS to treat all its freelance trainers as suppliers and set up their details on the purchase ledger system. Invoices can be entered on a weekly basis and payment made on a monthly basis.

Preferably the system should produce remittance advices. It may also print cheques, although the high cost of printing cheques is not acceptable to CTS at present. The staff salaries can be prepared on a manual payroll.

The nominal ledger should accept entries direct from the purchase ledger, but the sales information will have to be input by journal. A cash book module would deal with receipts and payments and the bank reconciliation. Reporting from the accounting system will be simple monthly income and expenditure (profit and loss) reports and a balance sheet. If the system can take the budget information and produce the comparisons, then fine. Otherwise, this would not be difficult to set up on a spreadsheet.

Needs assessment – example questions

How many transactions do we need to process in a month, e.g. number of purchase invoices, number of receipts and payments?

Do we need to invoice customers for income?

Do we sell any goods or services on credit?

Do we only supply after cash received?

How many activities or areas of work do we have?

How many sources of income do we have?

Is our main source of income unsolicited donations?

How many expenditure categories do we have in our budget?

How many regular suppliers do we have?

How many cost centres?

Are we likely to expand in the future – will it mean more cost centres?

How many staff do we have and how do we prepare the payroll?

What sort of reports do we want and how frequently?

Do we need different reports for different people?

Preparing a specification

The next stage is to write a clear specification of what the organisation wants from the system. It may not be able to get everything it wants from a package, and may have to compromise somewhere. However, it is still better to start from what you want. You can then measure each package you look at against your specification. You can also send your specification to dealers and ask whether they can supply a package that meets most of the points. It is also a good way of asking different dealers to cost out a package for you. At least you are comparing similar products.

Choosing a package

Using the needs assessment and specification, you are now ready to look at packages. Whilst there may be a great number on the market, you will be able to eliminate some of them very quickly. You should then look more closely at a shortlist of two or three.

It is useful to find out from the dealer or manufacturer how many other organisations similar to your own are using the software. It is often worthwhile to take up references with existing users, as you usually find out more about the support and maintenance that way. If you can find another similar organisation using the software, ask if you can visit. An on-site demonstration and a short conversation about how the organisation has found the software will give you more information than a pile of brochures.

Support is very important, as your needs may change. This is increasingly important as your organisation grows and your computer systems become more complex. You need to check that the company providing the support is well established and will continue for the foreseeable future. There are numerous stories of support companies going out of business, being bought out or losing interest in the particular software you have purchased. It is not always wise to go for the cheapest option.

Look at sample reports and print outs from the system and check whether the formats will be suitable or can be easily adapted. You may be able to export the data from the accounting software to a spreadsheet package and therefore design your own reports more easily. (Check for any additional cost involved.)

You may have to compromise on some of the points in your specification, so it is best to identify the most important ones and give those priority in your selection process.

Be sure to cost in all aspects of the computerisation process before you make your choice:

■ new hardware or upgrades

■ the software

- installation and set up

- software maintenance and support

- training.

You need to be sure that you have sufficient funds to complete the process – it is not sensible to buy a 'better' package and then find you cannot afford to train anyone to use it. You may have to compromise because of shortage of funds. If your organisation is *really* short of money, then think again. Is computerising the accounts the most important thing to do just now? Perhaps the money could be spent in better ways. Avoid mistakes at the other extreme as well – there is no point in buying a package just because it is cheap. If it does not match up to the most important points on your specification then it will not be able to do the job. You will be no better off with a computerised system; in fact it could cost you dearly if the accountant/auditor has to do a lot of additional work at the end of the year.

Choosing accounting software – example questions

- Can the system provide cost centre accounting?

- Can it produce separate reports for different managers?

- Can it produce reports in different ways for different purposes?

- Can it produce reports for funders?

- Can it be adapted to produce proper charity accounts that comply with the SORP?

- Can it track restricted, unrestricted and endowment funds?

- Can the system cope with the size of our organisation and complexity of accounts?

Implementation plan

A timetable needs to be thought through carefully and agreed with members of the organisation and possibly also outside people. The changeover to a new system may cause some disruption to payments, for example. Good communication is vital here, to ensure that you do not lose goodwill. You do not want everyone to blame the new system for everything, especially when it is really due to lack of human planning. You need to think about the work and time involved in installing a new system. Make room in your plan for things to go wrong, so that you can catch up and, overall, be on time with the whole implementation.

Illustration – Charity Training Services

CTS has chosen the software it wishes to use. It has identified the following tasks that need to be undertaken to implement the new system:

- Check names and addresses of existing customers

- Transfer existing customer details onto new database

- Set up records in database with necessary fields

- Write up existing manual cash book up to date

- Perform bank reconciliation up to date

- Prepare list of outstanding amounts due from customers and reconcile to a sales ledger control account

- Put details of courses onto database

- Put details of tutors and suppliers onto purchase ledger

- Set up nominal ledger accounts

- Enter test transactions and check output

- Set up reports required from database

- Set up reports required from accounting software

- Enter opening balances onto nominal ledger

- Inform tutors and other suppliers of change to new system

- Obtain banking details from tutors and suppliers so that payments can be made direct

- Circulate internal memo to explain implementation

- Conduct training sessions for finance staff

- Conduct training sessions for others

The above list is not in any particular order. The next task would be to check for completeness, then to organise this list into a timetable. If a number of staff are involved, then several tasks can be undertaken concurrently. The best way to work this out is to use a chart to plan the tasks, the timing and who should be doing what. If there are several people involved, they need to work as a team and a team leader should be in charge of the overall implementation. Team meetings will help to ensure that things go according to plan. If you are using consultants, it is important to agree the implementation plan and timetable with them. You will then need regular meetings to monitor the plan.

Note that many of the tasks on the list are not just about the new system; it is essential that your accounting records are up to date, balanced, checked and accurate *before* you put them onto the new system.

Testing

When you first get your new software, it is tempting to switch on and start using it on live data straight away. However, even after some training, you will still have a lot to learn about the new system and how you will be able to use it for your own organisation. It is much better, therefore, to set up a dummy organisation and enter some test data. If you have a system that will allow you to set up several companies, then set one up just for training and testing. Otherwise, check that you can install the software twice or ask your dealer for help. The best test will be to set up some real records and process some real transactions from a past month. This will help you to sort out how you want to reference transactions on the computer and what paperwork you will need to keep. How will you file paperwork? How will you mark it to show that it has been entered? How do you ensure that transactions do not get entered twice or missed? How will you check that the computer record is accurate?

Testing is an important part of the whole implementation. Even on well established accounting software packages, where you do not need to test the software as such, you need to test the operation for your own organisation. It is also a good opportunity to familiarise yourself with the package. All packages have little idiosyncrasies and it is better to find these out on some test data, rather than waste a lot of time using real data. Only when you are satisfied that the tests are satisfactory should you progress on to the next stage.

System operational

Having trained everyone and tested everything, you should finally be ready for the systems to be fully operational. It is useful to write your own operations manual as you go along. Although the software will usually have a manual, you may need to write something very simple for people in the organisation who only need to access information occasionally. This will also be useful for new staff. An operations manual will also include your own procedures and checks, not simply the computer-based functions. So, for example, the procedure for processing a purchase invoice from a supplier can include matching to the purchase order, checking for arithmetical accuracy and approval by the appropriate person.

Having established a system, it will need to be kept under review and developed as new demands are made on it.

PITFALLS TO AVOID

Computerising your accounts can save a lot of time and money; on the other hand, it can lead to a series of expensive mistakes. Some of the pitfalls to avoid:

Don't skimp on training – good systems are usually under-utilised and so the real benefits are missed because staff do not know how to use the system properly or to its full extent.

Don't skimp on software – a cheap but inappropriate package will be a waste of money, not a cost saving. Don't just buy for today, think ahead and buy for tomorrow.

Don't rush into setting up a system – you need to think through the whole operation and plan carefully. You do not have to start your new system at the beginning of the financial year; it is not a problem to transfer the balances onto the new nominal ledger. It is better to have prepared for the changeover properly, rather than to be in a muddle after the changeover.

Don't underestimate the time and effort a new system will require. It will take time for the benefits to be reaped.

Don't forget to set up appropriate controls and checks as part of the system. You still need to perform reconciliations on key control accounts and check reports.

Don't forget to set up good paper-based systems for controlling what goes into the computer. You will need to batch documents, set up checks to ensure they are entered once only and set up good filing systems.

Don't forget to set up a sensible referencing system so that transactions can be traced from one part of the system to another. This must include the paper records as well as the computer records.

Don't make adjustments to the accounting records without recording the reason for the entry. A system of numbered journal vouchers or forms to show the entry, the reason for it and the date and person making the entry is needed. Journal entries should also be authorised where there are several people in the department.

■ *Don't forget to make regular back-ups* of the information you have on the system.

OTHER CONSIDERATIONS

Cost centre accounting

Most charities will have different activities or projects and will need to keep track of the costs of individual projects. With the SORP on charity accounting, there will also be a need to identify restricted funds and keep track of expenditure on those individual funds. Additionally, many funders require reports on how their funds have been spent. This can lead to complicated accounting and reporting requirements for even quite small charities.

An accounting package needs to keep records in a way that runs parallel to your budget. This will usually involve a cost centre approach for incoming and outgoing resources. The nominal ledger will have to be designed so that the traditional income and expenditure accounts are there, such as salaries, rent, rates and insurance. In addition, the analysis should identify the project, activity or department that the income or expenditure item belongs to, such as motorbike workshop, fundraising, education. These are the cost centres.

Usually the coding system of the nominal ledger will allow you to code all the entries for the same cost centre with the same prefix or suffix. In a similar way, all entries for a particular account say, telephone, will have the same code. The nominal ledger can then sort the information by cost centre, by account or both. So you can have a report showing all the balances relating to a particular cost centre to give you information on a project's income and expenditure. You can also have a trial balance that shows the totals for all accounts without analysing into cost centres to give you the organisational income and expenditure account. You may also be able to get further reports, depending on the system. For preparation of accounts under the SORP, the cost centre report and the trial balance as described above are essential.

Some systems go further and can accommodate another analysis code. This may allow you to identify restricted and unrestricted funds. For some organisations, this may be essential if projects have funding from several sources, not all of which are restricted. Three-way analysis can be used in a number of ways in large organisations. Other systems allow you total flexibility in the nominal ledger structure and the cost centre accounting is simply a part of the list of accounts. For reports to be produced in the way you want, you have to build up the coding of the nominal ledger in the right way.

Cost centre accounting is likely to be essential for nearly all large charities. Obviously, for smaller charities with fewer projects, this may not be such a difficult issue. For larger charities with different sites, branches, projects and activities, it will be a major part of the planning exercise to design the nominal ledger structure, coding and reporting.

Accounting for VAT

For charities that are not registered for VAT, this will present no problems. Although the accounting software will allow you to analyse out the VAT, you ignore this and enter all expenditure inclusive of VAT.

For charities that are registered for VAT, the VAT on all expenditure should be analysed out when entered. Most charities are partially exempt for VAT purposes and so not all the VAT on purchases (input VAT) will be recoverable. Input VAT has to be identified to the different categories of VAT according to the activity to which the purchase relates. (See Chapter 10 for a VAT glossary and explanations of terms.) You need to keep several codes or accounts for input VAT as follows:

- Input VAT on purchases directly related to non-business activity

- Input VAT on purchases directly related to exempt activity

- Input VAT on purchases directly related to taxable activity

- Input VAT on purchases not directly related to a particular activity ('non-attributable')

This will enable you to extract the information you need for the preparation of the VAT return without too much further calculation. You will need to check whether the organisation is below the *de minimis* limit for partial exemption and calculate the proportion of the non-attributable VAT that may be recovered. The VAT account(s) should then be cleared down after the VAT return has been prepared. The amount recoverable or payable can be on the VAT control account, but the irrecoverable VAT should be transferred to an expenditure account ('written off'). It is usual to set up a separate account called 'Irrecoverable VAT' for this.

Security

It is important that accounting records and other information are safe from corruption and accessible only to those authorised to read them. Each user will have a password, which they have to type in before they can get into the system. You will be able to set up your system so that some areas are 'read only' to certain users. They may also be denied access entirely to certain areas. So sensitive information, such as salary details, can be accessible only to certain people. This system of passwords can also be used to ensure that only trained personnel can enter information onto the system or alter records. This would, for example, prevent anyone other than the payroll officer changing the salary rates.

The system also needs to be protected from corruption from computer viruses. If you operate a standalone personal computer or a small network without modem links, you can prevent viruses entering the system by prohibiting anyone from installing any of their own software onto the system. Staff should not be allowed to bring in their own programs (or games). Larger networks and computers using e-mail or the Internet should have virus-detecting software installed and regularly run.

Back-ups

You need to consider how you will back up information on the computer. You should think about what would happen in the event of a fire or a theft. (Remember, thieves often target the hard disk in your computer and leave the rest behind, so you would lose the essential part of your computer.)

Firstly, you should keep a back-up of the original disks containing the software in a safe place – either in a fire safe or on other premises. These may also be needed in the event of a hard disk failure.

Next you need to consider how you will keep regular back-ups of the data on the system. If there is a large volume of information and entries are made daily, then a back-up should be made at the end of every day. If you are a smaller user, you may consider a weekly back-up is sufficient. Remember, you are going to lose everything since your last back-up. It will be very time-consuming if you have to re-enter a lot of data.

Most computer users operate a 'grandfather, father, son' system. This means that you have three sets of back-up disks or tapes. At the end of day one, you use set A. At the end of day two, you use set B (leaving set A intact). At the end of day three, you use set C. At the end of day four you use set A again, overwriting the previous back-up. You then continue in this cyclical fashion. The idea behind this is that you have at least three chances of a good back-up! If data does become corrupted, it is possible that you would not notice immediately. So you could restore your data from set C, but this would have the corrupted data on it. You would then need to go back to set B or set A – hopefully, you would find uncorrupted data.

For accounting systems, it is usual to keep a permanent back-up for a complete year's transactions or some other convenient period.

SUMMARY

Computerised systems can certainly help your organisation to manage administration and finance more effectively. To achieve this, the systems have to be properly planned and implemented. You also have to have adequate funds to install and maintain all the systems, as well as train staff, to a sufficient standard.

9 Tax and trading

One of the main advantages of charitable status is the tax relief that is available to charities. Charities are exempt from income tax, corporation tax and capital gains tax on all income applied for charitable purposes. Additionally, charities do not pay stamp duty on transactions, e.g. the purchase of property. Charities also receive 80 per cent relief on business rates for the premises occupied by the charity, which may be extended to 100 per cent relief at the discretion of the local authority. Charities may also reclaim tax on gifts (covered in more detail in Chapter 11) and obtain some relief from VAT (covered in more detail in Chapter 10).

These tax reliefs will be forfeited if the charity is in breach of the special conditions attached to them. Certainly charities which trade will need to consider how they should structure their activities to avoid loss of valuable tax reliefs and to minimise the cost of tax on potentially taxable activities.

Charities must also consider the legal implications of straying too far into trading, as this may mean that the trustees are acting in breach of the charity's governing instrument. We will first look at the legal position of charities in relation to trading.

CHARITY TRADING AND THE LAW

A charity trading in the course of carrying out its main objective is quite legitimate and is known as primary purpose trading. Primary purpose or charitable trading will include the activities of charities that charge a fee for a service, such as nursing homes and schools, as well as the sale of goods produced by a charity's beneficiaries.

Secondary trading is not so straightforward and usually refers to trading to raise funds, such as the sale of Christmas cards. The charity first has to buy the cards in order to sell them. The purchase of the cards is not likely to be an application of funds within the charity's main objects. Thus, although the reason for the fundraising activity may be to generate funds for the main charitable purpose, this is too remote. The charity is undertaking commercial trading activities, which is not generally permitted under charity law. Substantial non-charitable trading may have to be channelled through another vehicle, such as a trading subsidiary.

Charities are allowed to carry on ancillary trading. Examples include such activities as selling refreshments to visitors to an art gallery, or providing childcare facilities to people attending a training course, both of which are services ancillary to the main event.

Infrequent fundraising events with a clear fundraising purpose are exempt from taxation, and traditional forms of fundraising such as public collections or flag days are not trading. The sale of donated goods (in charity shops and at functions, jumble sales etc.) is not treated as trading, but is seen as the conversion of donations into cash. Small-scale non-charitable trading will also be ignored, where this is insignificant compared with the charitable trading activities and in absolute amounts. The legal view on what is small-scale trading has been aligned with the HM Revenue & Customs (HMRC) guidance on this aspect and is therefore examined in more detail below.

CHARITY TRADING AND TAX

Certain sources of income, including investment income, interest received and rent received, are exempt from tax and are not considered trading. HMRC treats such income as income derived from the charity's assets, but not trading as such, so it is exempt from tax under a clause in the relevant legislation. A similar situation has been established for the sale of donated goods, seen as the conversion of goods into cash, but still the receipt of a donation. The implications for VAT are slightly different and care must be taken as the VAT rules for business activities are not the same as the tax rules on trading activities.

Charities are exempt from paying corporation tax, income tax or capital gains tax providing the income is applied for charitable purposes. (The main legislation giving the exemption is contained in section 505 of the Income and Corporation Taxes Act (ICTA) 1988.) HMRC does ask to see the accounts of charities periodically to check that the income is being applied for charitable purposes. This will be triggered by HMRC issuing a notice requiring completion of a corporation tax return CT600. Note that a penalty of £100 may be charged if a company fails to make a return if requested, or sends it in late (a company has 12 months after the financial year end in which to file the return).

The exemption is extended to trading profits used for charitable purposes including:

- the trade carrying out the primary purpose of the charity

- the trades undertaken by the beneficiaries of the charity

- ancillary trading.

Definition of trading

The definition of trading in the legislation is not very helpful; however, numerous cases have been to court over the question of whether a trade exists and so a body of law has been built up. The main points HMRC looks for are:

Repetition – where the trading is regular rather than a one-off event.

Profit motive – generally the profit motive should be present for trading to exist, even though a profit is not always actually made.

Mechanism for selling – the existence of a shop or catalogue or other means for the sale of the goods or services indicates the existence of a trade.

Acquisition of items for resale – buying goods with the intention of reselling rather than consuming them will indicate a trade.

HMRC could decide that a trade is being undertaken even if only one of the above criteria is fulfilled. It is unwise to rely on your own interpretation of the facts to decide that your organisation is not trading and therefore will not be liable to tax.

Primary purpose trading

Primary purpose trading is exempt from tax under s.505(1)(e) of ICTA 1988. Primary purpose trading is trading carried out in fulfilment of the charity's objects. For example:

The provision of educational services by a school or college in return for course fees.

The holding of an exhibition by an art gallery or museum in return for admission fees.

The sale of tickets for a theatrical production staged by a theatre.

The provision of healthcare services by a hospital in return for payment.

The provision of serviced residential accommodation by a residential care home in return for payment.

The sale of certain educational goods by an art gallery or museum.

If a trade is partly primary purpose and partly non-primary purpose then it is said to be a *mixed trade* (see below). An example is a gallery shop selling educational goods together with commemorative goods such as mugs and tea towels.

Trading undertaken mainly by the charity's beneficiaries

The profits of a trade are exempt where the work in connection with the trade is mainly carried out by beneficiaries of the charity. This often applies where the work carried out by the beneficiaries has a therapeutic, remedial or educational value. The trade itself need not be a primary purpose trade and the beneficiaries can be paid or unpaid. Examples include:

  A farm operated by students of an agricultural college.

  A restaurant operated by students as part of a catering course at a further education college.

  The sale of goods manufactured by disabled people who are beneficiaries of a disability charity.

'Mainly' means that the beneficiaries undertake at least 50 per cent of the work connected with the trade. In practice HMRC has usually taken a pragmatic approach when assessing whether the work is mainly undertaken by the beneficiaries, though case law has tended to be less lenient. If the beneficiaries carry out less than 50 per cent of the work then it is a mixed trade (see below).

Ancillary trading

Trading which is ancillary to a primary purpose is also exempt. Ancillary means that the trade is undertaken in the course of carrying out a primary purpose. HMRC quotes the following examples:

  The sale of relevant goods, or provision of services, for the benefit of students by a school or college (text books, for example).

  The provision of a crèche for the children of students by a school or college in return for payment.

  The sale of food and drink in a cafeteria to visitors to exhibits by an art gallery or museum.

  The sale of food and drink in a restaurant or bar to members of the audience by a theatre.

  The sale of confectionery, toiletries and flowers to patients and their visitors by a hospital.

However, if the trade deals in a range of goods or services, only some of which are within, or ancillary to, a primary purpose or if the trade deals with some customers who cannot properly be regarded as beneficiaries of the charity, the trade is not ancillary but mixed (see below). HMRC quotes the following examples:

  A shop in an art gallery or museum which sells a range of goods, some of which are related to a primary purpose of the charity (i.e. education and the preservation of property for the public benefit), for example direct reproductions of exhibits and catalogues, and some of which are not, for example promotional pens, mugs, tea towels and stamps.

The letting of serviced accommodation for students in term-time (primary purpose), and for tourists out of term-time (non-primary purpose), by a school or college.

The sale of food and drink in a theatre restaurant or bar both to members of the audience (beneficiaries of the charity) and the general public (non-beneficiaries).

Small-scale trading exemption

Since April 2000, trading activities have been allowed within charities up to specified limits:

if turnover from that activity is less than £5,000 in the year

if the turnover from the trade is less than 25 per cent of the gross income of the charity, or under £50,000, whichever is the lower.

This means that charities with a small operation selling Christmas cards or similar activities will be allowed to undertake the activities through the charity.

Profits may still be exempt if the charity can show that, at the start of the relevant accounting period, it was reasonable for it to expect that the turnover would not exceed the limit. This might be because:

■ the charity expected the turnover to be lower than it turned out to be, or

the charity expected that its total incoming resources would be higher than they turned out to be.

HMRC Charities will consider any evidence the charity may have to satisfy the reasonable expectation test. The charity will need to provide evidence to demonstrate the levels of turnover and incoming resources that were expected, for example minutes of meetings at which such matters were discussed, copies of cashflow forecasts, business plans and previous years' accounts.

Fundraising activities

As an extra statutory concession, HMRC allows charities to undertake small fundraising activities without incurring tax liabilities. The types of activities listed as examples are 'bazaars, jumble sales, gymkhanas, carnivals, firework displays'. In practice, the exemption will be extended to all small-scale fundraising events providing:

the charity is not regularly carrying out these trading activities

the trading is not in competition with other traders

■ the activities are supported substantially because the public is aware that any profits will be donated to charity

■ the profits are applied for charitable purposes.

In addition, there is a general exemption from tax (and VAT) for fundraising events. Charities may hold up to 15 events of the same kind in the same location in one financial year. Events may be held by the charity or its trading subsidiary, but the limit of 15 would apply to them jointly. Once you have 16 events, then you have lost the exemption altogether. Events can be widely interpreted, and so could include an event on the Internet or participatory events such as golf days.

Events have to be organised with a clear fundraising purpose, which should be made known to the public. Any events which create a distortion of competition and place a commercial enterprise at a disadvantage will not be exempt fundraising events.

Small-scale events can be ignored, as long as the aggregate gross takings from events of that type in that location do not exceed £1,000 in a week. This means that jumble sales and coffee mornings are not included when counting up the number of events.

Non-charitable voluntary organisations

Some organisations, such as campaigning groups, are ineligible for charitable status, even though they operate in a similar way to charities and do not distribute profits. Because they do not have charitable status, these organisations do not qualify for tax exemptions and may find that they have to pay tax on any surplus at the end of the financial year. However, if such organisations have income from voluntary sources, then this is not trading and not taxable. This would include gifts, donations, legacies and grants. If the organisation has some trading activity, such as the sale of publications, then it is possible to prepare a tax computation for that activity. This should bring in the direct costs and a proportion of the overheads to arrive at the taxable profit figure. The taxable profit is often very low and so the tax payable is not significant. The organisation will, however, have to pay tax on interest earned and no exemption from this is available for non-charitable voluntary organisations.

Mixed trades

Where a trade is not entirely primary purpose or ancillary to the primary purposes and is not mainly carried out by the charity's beneficiaries, then the trade is said to be *mixed*. The rules on mixed trades were changed with effect from 22 March 2006 and now the two components (within the exemption and not covered by the exemption) are deemed to be two separate trades. The trade within the exemption is exempt, as long as its profits are used for charitable purposes. The trade deemed non-primary purpose is taxable, although the exemption for small trading can apply to this trade. Any receipts or expenses relating to the overall trade should be apportioned to the separate trades on a reasonable basis.

For example, a shop selling books and souvenirs may be selling books that are within the exemption because they are primary purpose, but the sale of souvenirs is deemed a separate trade. If this activity is undertaken within the charity, then the income from selling souvenirs should be within the small-scale trading exemption (see above).

You may need to calculate the taxable profits if the non-primary purpose trading is significant. HMRC guidance requires a 'reasonable apportionment of expenses and receipts'. This takes into account direct expenditure and a reasonable proportion of indirect expenditure such as overheads, whether or not these were originally incurred for charitable purposes. If losses arise from trading which is within the charitable objects of a charity, they will be regarded as charitable expenditure. If the losses arise from non-primary purpose trading they will be regarded as non-charitable expenditure.

Trading subsidiaries

The common way to deal with trading that does not fall within the exemptions is to channel the income and expenditure relating to those activities through a separate company. Usually the company will be an ordinary share company, with general trading objects and the usual clauses for a commercial undertaking. It is normal for two shares to be issued, which are usually owned by the charity, or by charity trustees who hold them on trust for the benefit of the charity. Either way, the charity should control the trading company and decide who the director(s) will be, thus making the company a subsidiary of the charity.

A company must have a minimum of one director, but usually there will be several. It is tempting to make all the trustees of the charity the directors of the trading company. However, this is unwise and the Charity Commission advises against it. If the two boards are exactly the same, there could be a conflict of interest. The charity trustees must always have regard to the interests of the beneficiaries of the charity and so must protect its assets and minimise risk. Whilst the trading subsidiary may wish to maximise profits for the benefit of the charity, there may be occasions where a conflict could arise, such as agreeing a management charge (a payment made by the company for the services of the charity, for example staff time) between the two organisations.

Many charities like to have some representation on the board of directors of the trading company, to ensure that they exercise control in practice as well as in theory. This may be one or two employees of the charity and one or two trustees. Preferably they should be people with business experience. It may also be appropriate to have one or two senior employees of the trading company on the board of directors, as one might in a commercial setting. It is worth remembering that the board of directors of a trading company does not have to be large. It is not the same as the board of trustees of a charity, where you may be trying to represent a number of interests.

The charity will need to review how the subsidiary is managed, once it is established. The trading subsidiary's AGM is an opportunity for the charity to receive a full report of the activities of the subsidiary over the past year and its plans for the next. The charity can ensure that the strategic objectives of the company are not in conflict with its own and that the return is satisfactory. This is part of the trustees' governance role and in keeping with their duty to monitor investments.

One of the benefits of channelling trading activities through a separate company is that it is possible to achieve a certain clarity of objectives. The main objective of a trading company is fundraising for the charity and it should be trying to maximise profits and the return on capital. It should therefore be measured by fairly standard commercial criteria. It is true that a certain amount of image enhancement or public profile may also be achieved, but this should not be used to justify loss-making trading activities. A charity is more likely to prop up a loss-making activity if it is kept under the charity umbrella, whereas this becomes harder to justify once the activity is hived off into a separate trading company.

Advantages of a separate trading subsidiary

■ Protects charity from tax liability

■ Clarifies objectives for each part of the organisation

■ Limited liability status for separate trading company may protect charitable funds in the event of a mistake

■ Allows you to undertake certain activities which a registered charity may not

■ May be convenient for VAT planning

Disadvantages of a separate trading subsidiary

■ A more complex structure with added costs, e.g. incorporation, audit, professional advice

■ Knowledge of very specific tax rules is needed

■ Company must operate at 'an arm's length' to the charity

- There may have to be management charges between company and charity

- Rate relief may be lost

Profit shedding

In order for the arrangement to work, the trading company must shed its taxable profits by tax-effective transfer to the charity. This is usually achieved by gift aid.

The trading subsidiary can make the gift aid payment to the charity up to nine months after the end of the company's financial year. The gift aid may be included in the trading subsidiary's corporation tax computation for the financial year. This gives the company time to draw up accounts and calculate the taxable profit.

The trading subsidiary can also make transfers at various points during the year by gift aid, and make a final payment after the end of the financial year to mop up the rest of the profit. This use of gift aid works in the same way as for any company and no forms or declarations are required. The amount paid to the charity is the gross amount and the charity does not claim back any tax. The trading subsidiary only has to enter the gift aid payment on its corporation tax return.

Financing the trading

Whatever the activity, there will be a need to consider how the activity will be financed. Working capital may be needed for stock, premises or equipment and therefore charitable funds may be needed to finance the start-up costs.

INVESTMENT POWERS If the charity uses its own funds to finance the initial working capital of the trading subsidiary, this amounts to an investment by the charity, and the rules on such an investment apply just as for any other investment. The charity must have the power to invest as part of its constitution. Note that if the charity does not have the appropriate power to invest, then it may not even buy a trading company, spend funds on setting one up or spend just £2 on the minimum of shares. If this is the case, the charity should amend its constitution and agree the amendment with the Charity Commission. The power to invest must be sorted out before the charity embarks on trading activities (see Chapter 4 for details).

COMMERCIAL LOAN Assuming the charity has investment powers, the trustees must give careful consideration to the decision to invest and the most appropriate way to fund the working capital. One option is to seek a commercial loan from a bank or similar lender. Commercial lenders will be reluctant to lend to a company that is really just a 'shell' – which is what the trading subsidiary of a charity will be

– and, because the company will be transferring all its profits to the charity, it will never have a very healthy balance sheet. It is also likely to have few assets, so the security for a commercial lender will be scant. It is therefore likely that the lender would seek guarantees from the charity. This presents difficulties for charities because trustees would probably be in breach of trust if a guarantee was called upon and the charity's assets were lost to satisfy the liabilities of the trading company. In addition, a commercial loan is an expensive way of funding the trading, since the company will be paying interest to a third party instead of paying it to the charity. If the charity has the spare funds to invest in the trading company, a commercial loan would be a wasteful course of action.

It may be possible to obtain cheaper loan finance from one of the sources being established to lend to charities. Often, the terms are not as onerous as normal commercial loans and the lenders may lend without the security of fixed assets. (See *Sources of further information*.)

LOAN FROM THE CHARITY The most common route for funding the working capital of the trading company is for the charity to lend the money to the company. This should be properly assessed, just as if the loan were to an external body. The trustees should receive appropriate documents, such as a business plan, to satisfy themselves that the trading is viable. The trustees' decision should be taken at a trustees' meeting and minuted. There should be a loan agreement, and commercial rates of interest should be charged. The interest should actually be paid over; it is not sufficient for an entry simply to be made in the accounting records. There should be a charge over the trading company's assets, including stock, debtors and cash balances (it is usual to take a fixed and floating charge). This has to be registered at Companies House and means that the charity has the power to appoint a receiver and has first call on the assets of the company should it become insolvent.

Remember the following key points when considering a loan to a trading company:

- Assess the loan request as if it were from an external body

- Document the decision

- Ensure that a business plan is drawn up

- Execute a loan agreement

- The trading company should pay a commercial rate of interest to the charity

- The charity should have charge over trading company's assets

SHARES The charity could buy more than the minimum number of shares in the trading company. This would provide the company with some or all of the capital needed to start up. The decision to buy share capital would have to be made in the same way as any other investment decision. The disadvantage with investment by shares is that the charity will have few ways of recouping its investment. The shareholders are the last to be paid out in the event of a winding up and the share capital cannot easily be repaid if the company continues trading. It is possible for the company to buy its own shares back, although this is unlikely to be possible in the situation where the profits are being passed up to the charity. The charity might be able to sell the company to a commercial purchaser at some point, but this is also an unlikely route. Hence, share capital more or less permanently ties up the charity's money, whereas there is the possibility that a loan might be repaid. Having said all that, it may well be the appropriate course of action for a trading company that wished to have a 'clean break' from the parent charity.

A trading company can retain profits to build up its reserves to cover its own working capital requirements; however, tax has to be paid on profits before they are retained.

Shared premises, facilities, staffing

If the trading company uses any facilities or staff time paid for by the charity, then a service charge or management charge must be made. The charity should charge these facilities at cost and will have to bear in mind that they will be subject to VAT if the charity exceeds the VAT threshold. Care must be taken that the principle of operating 'at arm's length' is maintained. Neither should the charity make a profit on the management services, unless they are primary purpose trading, as otherwise the profits may be taxable.

It is usually wiser for the charity to own the major fixed assets and lease these to the trading subsidiary, otherwise the charity would have to lend the money to the trading subsidiary and then take a fixed charge over the assets. It is therefore easier for the charity to retain ownership of all significant assets (certainly property) so that it is not risking those assets. However, the VAT position will also have to be considered, in order that VAT recovery may be maximised.

Setting up a trading company

Before you set up the trading company, ask yourselves the following questions:

- Do we need a trading company? Is our trading actually fulfilling the primary purpose of the charity or otherwise exempt from tax as small-scale trading, fundraising or fundraising events?

- Does our constitution allow us invest in the shares of a company?

- Which activities should be channelled through the trading company?

Do those activities make a profit? What would be the working capital needs of a trading company?

Can the charity afford to lend or invest the working capital or will the company have to go to a commercial lender?

Should some of the investment be share capital?

What will be the charity's return on the investment and is this adequate?

Will the company use facilities or staff time which the charity should charge for?

How will the VAT position be affected?

Having decided to go ahead, you need to:

Buy an off-the-shelf commercial company with general trading objects. Company formation agents have ready-formed companies which you can buy off the shelf. You need to allow about £300, and will need to change the company name.

Decide on the amount of the charity's investment, and whether this should be in the form of share capital, and allot shares accordingly.

Appoint directors of the company.

Inject some working capital and formalise any loans through proper loan agreements.

Ensure there are proper agreements if there are any arrangements for use of facilities, equipment and so on.

Set up systems to monitor profitability and liquidity.

Monitoring the profitability of the trading

It is obviously important that charities monitor the effectiveness of trading subsidiaries carefully. Because the main purpose of the company is to generate profits for the charity, commercial measures may be used to judge the company's performance.

Profitability should be measured against expectations. It can also be useful to compare your performance with that of other similar operations. However, it is difficult to get sufficient data as this sort of information can be commercially sensitive. More usually, you monitor the trends in performance by using certain ratios and comparisons with previous years or against budget. The ratios which may be useful are:

return on capital employed

gross profit percentage

stock turnover

age of debtors

creditor payment period.

Other measures used in the retail trade include:

turnover per staff member

turnover per square metre of retail space

Trading or fundraising?

Having set up a trading company, there will need to be clear rules about which activities are channelled through the trading company and which are carried out through the charity. Charitable trading may go through the charity, as may many fundraising activities, such as exempt events and lotteries. It is advantageous for shops selling donated goods to be kept within the charity, as then the charity retains eligibility to mandatory rates relief. However, shops selling a significant proportion of new goods will have to check the small-scale trading exemption and may need to channel activities through the trading company.

As well as considering the legal and tax issues, charities should also think about how the arrangements will be managed. It may be simpler to undertake all of one type of fundraising activity, such as events, through the trading subsidiary. There is no loss or additional cost to the charity, as profits may be transferred to the charity at regular intervals by gift aid.

Incoming funds that buy the funder some promotion or advertising are trading and should go through the trading company if the advertising is significant. However, sponsorship of an exempt fundraising event will be considered part of the income and therefore covered by the exemption.

Anti-avoidance legislation

A condition of tax relief is that the income must be spent on the charitable purposes and tax exemptions are not available for non-charitable expenditure. Non-charitable expenditure covers:

investments or loans that do not meet the requirements to be charitable investments or loans (see below)

losses on non-charitable trading or other non-charitable activities and losses on trades where any profit would not be exempt

expenditure that is not for charitable purposes

149

■ non-qualifying payments to a substantial donor or as a result of transactions with a substantial donor (this is covered in more detail in Chapter 11).

If a charity makes a non-qualifying investment this will count as non-qualifying expenditure in the year that it is made, but will not affect subsequent years.

Qualifying investments include listed shares, unit trusts, commercial bank deposits, land and some other pooled investment funds. Qualifying investments also include other investments that HMRC accepts are for the benefit of the charity; qualifying loans are similarly defined. HMRC guidance on acceptability states that loans will bear a commercial rate of interest and have suitable security and repayment terms. In practice the most common area of difficulty for investments and loans relates to the financing of subsidiaries. For example, a charity makes a loan of £100,000 to its trading subsidiary. The loan is unsecured and does not specify a rate of interest or repayment terms. This counts as non-charitable expenditure of £100,000 on the date the loan is made.

The consequence of this is that an equivalent amount of charitable trading income will lose its exempt status. You then have to attribute expenditure to the activity, apportion overheads and calculate the profit or loss on the activity. Tax is payable where there is a profit and loss relief may be available under normal corporation or income tax rules if there is a loss.

Particular trades

SALE OF DONATED GOODS The sale of donated goods by a charity is generally not regarded as a trade for tax purposes, but as the realisation of the value of a gift. This is so even where the donated items are sorted, cleaned and given minor repairs. If the goods are subjected to significant refurbishment or to any process which brings them into a different condition for sale purposes from that in which they were donated, the sale proceeds may be regarded as trading income.

LETTINGS All rental income from land or buildings received by a charity is exempt from tax provided the profits arising are applied for charitable purposes. However, if services are provided along with the use of the land or buildings (for example, provision of a caretaker, food or laundry) these in themselves might amount to trading. Letting activity will itself constitute a trade where the owner remains in occupation of the property and provides services over and above those usually provided by a landlord. Essentially the distinction lies between the hotelier (who is carrying on a trade) and the provider of furnished accommodation (who is not). An important difference is that in a hotel. the occupier of the room does not acquire any legal interest in the property. Each case must be considered on its own facts.

SPONSORSHIP Business sponsors may fund the general work of the charity or a particular charitable project. Sponsorship arrangements often link the name of the business with the charity or its project, creating in the minds of the public an affinity between the business and the charity. The affinity with charity created by sponsorship is a valuable marketing asset for businesses. However, just because a sponsor derives good publicity or public relations benefits from payments to charity, does not auto matically mean that the payments are trading income in the hands of the charity. If the charity does not provide goods or services in return for payment, sponsorship payments will normally have the character of charitable donations rather than trading income in the charity's hands.

The fact that the business sponsor takes steps to publicise or exploit the affinity with the charity will not change the treatment of the payments in the hands of the charity, unless the charity also publicises the affinity itself. Usually a charity will play a part in publicising the business sponsor's affinity by including references to the sponsor in publications, posters, etc. and at events organised by the charity. Provided that such references amount to no more than acknowledgement of the sponsor's contributions they will not cause the payments to be regarded as trading income. However, references to a sponsor which amount to advertisements will cause the payments to be treated as trading income.

It is recognised that where a sponsor's funding is tied to a particular event or project, it may not be practical to confine the charity's response to a mere acknowledgement. However, any arrangement in which the charity's response is on such a scale that it appears to be a main purpose of the donation may be challenged. In such a case, HMRC will want to consider the possibility of non-primary purpose trading by the charity and whether there has been a breach of the donor's benefits limits.

USE OF A CHARITY'S LOGO Payments solely for the use of a charity's logo will generally be classified as non-trading gains on intangible fixed assets. Non-trading gains on intangible fixed assets received by charitable companies are exempt as long as the gains are applied charitably. Where a charity allows its logo to be used by a business, in return for payment, as an endorsement for one or more of the business's products or services, and the charity likewise promotes the endorsement in its own literature, the payments are likely to be trading income of the charity.

AFFINITY CREDIT CARDS A charity may receive payments from a bank, building society or other financial institution in return for endorsing that institution's credit card and recommending its use to the charity's members or supporters. Such cards are normally referred to as affinity credit cards.

The direct tax treatment follows the VAT treatment. Any payment accepted as a true donation for VAT purposes would normally be accepted as such for tax purposes.

Anything else paid to the charity in relation to the affinity card is likely to be taxable non-primary purpose trading income.

Subject to the agreements between the charity and the card provider being structured in a qualifying manner, the bulk of the monies received by a charity from the card provider can be treated as outside the scope of VAT. A typical qualifying agreement between the charity and the card provider will provide for the supply by the former (or its trading subsidiary) to the latter of the following services:

- Access to the charity's membership or mailing lists and/or mailing of the card provider's promotional literature to members.

- Endorsement of the card and marketing of the card by the charity to its members/supporters.

- The right to use the charity's name and logo on the card and on the card provider's promotional literature.

Typically a card provider will pay an agreed amount to the charity (or its trading subsidiary) on the issue of each new card. Thereafter the card provider pays the charity a percentage of the turnover (value of purchases) on the card. The basis of the relief is that payments by card providers to a charity, made solely in respect of the use of the charity's name and logo, can be treated as contributions for which the charity is not obliged to do anything in return. To benefit from this treatment there must be two separate agreements:

- One agreement, between the charity (or its trading subsidiary) and the card provider should allow for the supply by the charity (or its trading subsidiary) of the necessary marketing and publicity services, access to membership lists and other promotional activity for the card (marketing services). These supplies are taxable at the standard rate.

- A second and separate agreement between the charity and the card provider should allow for contributions to be made by the card provider in respect of the use only of the charity's name and/or logo. Contributions made under this agreement can be treated as outside the scope.

This being the case, part (at least 20 per cent) of the initial payment can be treated as the consideration for the standard-rated business supplies by the charity. The remaining 80 per cent (or less) of the initial payment, and all subsequent payments based on turnover, will be outside the scope of VAT.

SUMMARY

Charities with many creative fundraising ideas will need to be alert to the tax implications of their efforts. Good communication between fundraisers and sound financial management is essential to ensure that clearance for the new activity is obtained before it begins. It is often impossible to arrange matters to be tax-effective after the event, whereas considerable benefits may accrue to the charity if events are well-planned and the available reliefs used properly.

10 VAT

Glossary of VAT terminology

Business activities	Defined by VAT law as the exchange of goods or services for value.
Non-business activities	Supplies made with no commercial intent, such as voluntary donations.
Outside the scope	Certain activities are not covered by the VAT regime, principally employment (salaries are not subject to VAT) and non-business transactions.
Exempt	Certain business activities do not carry any VAT because they are on a list of exempt goods or services, e.g. health services.
Taxable	The two categories of zero-rated and standard-rated come under a group of taxable activities.
Zero-rated	Certain business activities are taxable, but carry VAT at zero rate.
Standard-rated	VAT must be charged by VAT-registered businesses at 17.5 per cent (currently).
Input VAT	The VAT on business purchases which may be recovered by offsetting against output VAT.
Output VAT	The VAT you charge on sales and which you have to collect from customers. You then pay this over to HM Revenue & Customs (HMRC) (after deducting input VAT you have paid out on purchases).

INTRODUCTION

VAT is a sales tax charged by businesses on the goods and services they supply, except very small businesses whose turnover is below the VAT threshold. The threshold is usually revised upwards at the beginning of each tax year; the current threshold can be checked out on the HMRC website (see *Sources of further information*). Whilst many charities have gross income exceeding the threshold, many of them are not registered for VAT.

It is also widely assumed that charities are exempt from paying VAT as part of the tax reliefs available to charities. This is far from being the case: VAT actually costs charities millions of pounds each year, because they pay VAT when they purchase goods and services, just as ordinary individuals do.

Business or non-business

The reason why charities are often not registered for VAT is that they are not undertaking *business* activities. If they are not registered for VAT, then they cannot charge VAT, nor may they recover VAT. Activities such as collecting donations or undertaking grant-funded work will always be non-business activities and therefore *outside the scope* of VAT. On the other hand, charities frequently undertake activities which do fall within the scope of VAT. However, some business activities are *exempt* from VAT, and some may be *zero-rated*, so VAT will not be chargeable on all business income.

A certain amount of planning can be undertaken before an activity commences, to arrange things to the benefit of the charity. The VAT rules are not, however, flexible and care must be taken. If in doubt, you should always contact your local VAT office to obtain a ruling for your specific situation.

Note that only VAT registered traders may recover VAT, and then only on their *business* activities.

REGISTERING FOR VAT

To register for VAT, you must complete a form and obtain a VAT registration number, which must be quoted on all sales invoices.

A business must register for VAT when it exceeds the VAT threshold. This is measured on a 'rolling' 12-month period. So, at the end of any month, if you look back over the previous year and income from *taxable* business activities exceeds the threshold, you should register for VAT. You have a month to obtain and complete a form and you should start charging VAT from the effective date of registration stated on your VAT certificate. You must quote your VAT registration number on all invoices. Note that VAT cannot be charged retrospectively – the VAT threshold is a trigger for registration and you can only start charging VAT once you are registered. You may recover some VAT on purchases (*input VAT*) incurred prior to registration; this would include purchases of goods up to one year prior to registration and services up to six months prior to registration. However, these would have to be purchases for business activity. (See section on VAT recovery.)

You should also register if you see that you will exceed the threshold in the next 30 days.

Registration is also possible for new enterprises which are likely to have to register compulsorily at a later date. You may have to give evidence of contracts or business plans to support your case for registration from the point that the business is established. Since you will usually be claiming back VAT on setting up costs, HMRC will retain the right to claw back VAT paid to the business if turnover does not exceed the registration threshold by the end of the first year. This is an anti-avoidance measure.

Voluntary registration

You may also register for VAT even if your taxable supplies are below the threshold. Note that you must have *some* taxable supplies. Registration is advantageous because you can recover VAT on purchases relating to the taxable activity. You will need to consider carefully who will be paying the VAT – remember it is the end consumer who finally pays. So to register for VAT and start charging VAT on, for example, admission fees would effectively be an increase in the price of admission for the public.

VAT categories of supplies

In order to establish whether the charity should register for VAT, you need to go through your sources of income and identify which VAT category they belong to:

- non-business

- exempt

- taxable, further sub-divided into:

    - zero-rated

    - reduced-rated

    - standard-rated.

Non-business supplies

These will usually be 'one-way' transactions, where something is given without an expectation that it will be reciprocated. Voluntary donations and grants are income to the charity that comes into the non-business category. So will welfare activities, where the contribution paid by a beneficiary is minimal. The rule is that the charity should be subsidising the activity by at least 15 per cent of the total cost. So many centres providing meals and drinks where a small charge is made will come into this category, as they receive grants and donations to subsidise the service. Non-business supplies are not subject to VAT and do not count towards the registration threshold.

Exempt supplies

These are activities that are specified as exempt by VAT legislation. They include broad categories such as health and education, including many charities' charitable activities. The following activities will be exempt for VAT purposes:

- medical care by recognised professionals

- education in schools, universities, colleges

- vocational training courses run by eligible bodies, which includes charities and some other not-for-profit bodies (vocational meaning that the training should help people in their paid or voluntary work and can include educational conferences)

- nursing homes, registered care homes, hospices

- registered nurseries, crèches, playgroups and youth club activities

- renting out residential accommodation

- welfare services

- fundraising events run by charities.

There are further specific exemptions for certain activities; the above list is not exhaustive. Fundraising events are covered in more detail later in this chapter.

Exempt supplies are not subject to VAT and do not count towards the registration threshold.

Zero-rated supplies

Some activities are taxable, but at zero rate. These are listed in a schedule to the VAT legislation, which is amended from time to time. There are some broad areas which apply to everyone, such as unprepared food and children's clothing. There are also some activities that are zero-rated when undertaken by charities. The following activities are zero-rated supplies:

sales of publications, including magazines and newsletters

sales of children's clothes and shoes

sale of food (not take-aways)

exports

sales of donated goods by a charity or its subsidiary.

The turnover on these activities will count towards the VAT threshold when considering the need for registration. It also means that charities with some of these activities can voluntarily register for VAT.

Reduced-rated supplies

Some activities are subject to VAT at a reduced rate. In most cases this will only affect charities as purchasers. Fuel and power are supplied at a reduced rate of VAT of 5 per cent to domestic users and charities if they are using the fuel for non-business purposes. This also entitles the customer to relief from paying the Climate Change Levy. Only registered suppliers can apply the reduced rate of VAT to supplies, so charities may receive supply at this reduced rate, but will not be able to make supplies at this rate.

Standard-rated supplies

Most sales of goods and services will be standard-rated, even if they are supplied by a charity. This includes many fundraising activities that involve some sort of merchandising or sales. It is safest to assume that an activity will be standard-rated unless you can establish that it is non-business, exempt or zero-rated.

Standard-rated and zero-rated supplies together count towards the threshold for VAT registration. Voluntary registration will be an option for charities with some standard-rated supplies, although this would mean they would also have to charge VAT on the standard-rated activity.

VAT categories for certain activities

Some of the activities undertaken by charities need further consideration in order to establish their VAT category.

WELFARE Welfare services cover the following supplies:

care, treatment or instruction designed to promote physical or mental welfare of older, sick, distressed (see below) or disabled people

care and protection of children or young people

spiritual welfare provided by a religious institution as part of a course of instruction or a retreat, not being designed primarily to provide recreation or a holiday.

Charities that provide welfare services at significantly below cost, 'to distressed persons for the relief of their distress', may treat these supplies as non-business and therefore outside the scope of VAT. 'Significantly below cost' means subsidised by at least 15 per cent and the subsidy must be available to everyone. The charity must be providing the service to distressed individuals and not a local authority. 'Distressed' means someone who is suffering pain, grief, anguish, severe poverty etc.

Welfare services provided by a charity, public body or 'state-regulated private welfare institution or agency' are exempt from VAT. This means that there is no longer a category of exempt welfare provided by a not-for-profit body. Welfare services will be exempt if they are regulated under care standards or a similar body. The activities and services caught by this are:

  registered care homes

  domiciliary care – home helps

  registered nurseries and crèches

  foster and adoption agencies.

Some charities had been undertaking these activities in a trading subsidiary, so that they would be able to charge VAT. This is no longer an effective strategy, even if the services are provided under contract to a local authority.

ADMISSION CHARGES AND CULTURAL ACTIVITIES Admission charges to many events and performances are standard-rated; however, charities may be covered by the cultural exemption. This means that, under certain circumstances, admission charges to museums, galleries, art exhibitions and zoos, and theatrical, musical or choreographic performances of a cultural nature are exempt from VAT when provided by a public authority or eligible body To qualify as an eligible body an organisation must satisfy three tests:

  It must be non-profit-making.

  It must apply any profits made from exempt admission fees to the continuance or improvement of the facilities made available by means of the supplies.

  It must be managed and administered on an essentially voluntary basis by people who have no direct or indirect financial interest in the activities of the body.

Non-profit-making – an organisation that does not systematically aim to make a profit and which, if profits do arise, must not distribute them. A body whose constitution or articles of association preclude it from distributing surpluses of income over expenditure to its members, shareholders or any other party (other than in the event of a liquidation or cessation of activities), and which as a matter of fact does not distribute any profit, will normally be accepted as having satisfied this condition.

Any profits are applied towards the cultural services – all profits arising from exempt admission fees must be used:

- for the continuance or improvement of the facilities made available to the fee-paying public by payment of the exempt admission fees, or

- applied in connection with the making of related cultural supplies (such as research or conservation projects).

If profits are applied to any other activities of the body than those above, the body is not eligible for exemption.

Managed and administered on an essentially voluntary basis – the key test comprises two separate tests, both of which must be satisfied for the cultural exemption to apply. The body must be:

- *Managed on an essentially voluntary basis* – if someone is paid for their role as a board member, and this is not a nominal, token or one-off payment and the person genuinely plays an active role on the board and takes part in important decisions, then this will preclude management on an essentially voluntary basis.

- *By people who have no direct or indirect financial interest in the activities of the body* – having a direct or indirect financial interest means being able to profit from the success of the organisation (e.g. by bonuses) or to extract profits (e.g. by being paid an excessive salary). A market rate salary does not constitute financial interest. An interest in this context means a beneficial interest. A trustee underwriting a potential loss is not a financial interest – the financial interest has to be potentially beneficial in a positive sense (i.e. not that the trustee could avoid making a loss but that he/she stands to gain in some way).

MEMBERSHIP SUBSCRIPTIONS Many charities operate a membership subscription as a means of both fundraising and building awareness of the objects of the charity. Membership subscriptions can be treated in different ways for VAT. They can be:

- exempt

- non-business (outside the scope of VAT)

- taxable i.e. subject to standard or zero-rate VAT

- a mixture of some or all of the above.

Subscriptions are presumed to be exempt where the only benefits are those such as the right to vote at the AGM and to receive the annual report. This applies to non-profit-making organisations whose aims are in the public domain and are of a political, religious, patriotic, philosophical, philanthropic or civic nature. Such bodies may or may not be charitable. The subscriptions of trades unions and professional bodies were already classified as exempt.

However, membership schemes that are simply a means of raising donations will be classified as non-business and therefore outside the scope of VAT. In this situation there will be no benefits.

The VAT treatment depends on the VAT status of the benefits of membership. An extra-statutory concession allows not-for-profit organisations to agree with HMRC an apportionment of the subscription, and so treat the subscription as a multiple supply of the various benefits, with each carrying its applicable VAT or exempt status. Each benefit has to be valued individually, based on the cost to your organisation of providing the benefit. So, for example, if you provide a magazine, you have to work out the cost of producing and circulating it. You then work out the cost of zero-rated and standard-rated benefits and assume everything else is exempt.

You need to agree the apportionment basis with your local VAT office before it can be applied, and monitor changes in the package of benefits being offered to members. You also need to monitor the impact on the VAT recovery and factor this into the annual adjustment at the end of the tax year.

Example – Membership subscriptions

Membership benefits amount to a free magazine issued four times a year (costing £2.50 per issue to produce and send out) and a discount on tickets for performances worth approximately £2 per ticket. The overall discounts given last year, according to the accounting records, totalled £24,000. Since there are 3,000 members, this is the equivalent of each member benefiting from annual discounts of £8. The membership subscription is £35 per year. The apportionment could be calculated as follows:

Magazine	£10	Zero-rated benefit
Discount on tickets	£8	Standard-rated benefit
Balance = donation	£17	Outside the scope

The optimum position is achieved by increasing the zero-rated element of a subscription. This means that all input VAT relating to membership can be recovered, whilst the output VAT is zero.

SPONSORSHIP There is a significant difference between a corporate *donation* and corporate *sponsorship*. If a donation is received, then nothing should be given to the company in return. Sponsorship, on the other hand, is a reciprocal arrangement. The company receives advertising or promotional services in return for the cash given to the charity. Sponsorship is therefore a *business* arrangement and is standard-rated. It is also potentially liable to corporation tax because it is trading income. Consequently, some advance planning is needed for this type of fundraising and most charities set up a separate trading company for this and other business income. The trading company is usually registered for VAT right from the beginning.

Alternatively, the company could give a donation to the charity, possibly under gift aid or a covenant, and receive no benefits in return. The charity may simply acknowledge the gift in the annual report, which would be outside the scope of VAT.

It may be possible to sell some advertising or promotional services to a company, charging an appropriate fee, as well as receive a donation. It is essential that this sort of arrangement is set up beforehand as it cannot be constructed retrospectively.

Charities are also often engaged in cause-related marketing. This is where the company uses the charity's name and logo to help sell a product. The charity should sell the right to use its name and logo under a licence agreement, which is potentially a standard-rated activity if the charity needs to be registered for VAT. The company may also agree to donate monies to the charity, which would be outside the scope of VAT.

FUNDRAISING EVENTS Fundraising events held by charities and wholly owned subsidiaries are exempts from VAT. They do not have to be one-off – charities may have up to 15 events of the same kind in the same location in one financial year. Events may be held by the charity or its trading subsidiary, or jointly by several charities, but the limit of 15 would apply jointly. Once you have 16 events, you have lost the exemption. Events can be widely interpreted, so they include events on the Internet and participatory events such as golf days.

Such events must be organised with a clear fundraising purpose, which should be made known to the public. Any events that create a distortion of competition and place a commercial enterprise at a disadvantage will not be exempt fundraising events.

Small-scale events can be ignored, as long as the aggregate gross takings from events of that type in that location do not exceed £1,000 in a week. This means, for example, that jumble sales and coffee mornings are not included when counting up the number of events.

If you are unsure whether an event will be covered by the exemption, speak to your local VAT office before you organise it. If it is exempt for VAT, it will also be exempt from direct tax.

The exemption applies to all income at the event, including sponsorship. However, income that would normally be zero-rated, such as the sale of printed matter or donated goods, can continue to be zero-rated, allowing full recovery of associated input VAT.

Participatory events will only be included in the exemption if they do not provide any accommodation or the accommodation is incidental, which means no more than two nights. This effectively rules out most overseas challenge events as they involve more than two nights' accommodation. These events usually involve the payment of an entry or registration fee. If the event qualifies as a fundraising event the fee will not subject to VAT. Note that the event must be organised by a charity or its subsidiary to qualify for the exemption. The amounts raised as 'sponsorship' are covered by the exemption from VAT.

Problems have arisen with the London Marathon because it is organised by a for-profit company rather than a charity, even though it involves so much fundraising. Thus it cannot qualify as a fundraising event and if a charity charges participants a registration or entry fee, this is subject to VAT. If the charity goes further and insists that the participant raises a minimum amount of sponsorship, this will also be subject to VAT. HMRC has clarified that it will accept that these amounts can be outside the scope of VAT and treated as donations if the charity only asks the participant to pledge an amount of sponsorship.

Charities usually buy 'gold-bond' places in the London Marathon – and these are subject to VAT. Charging VAT on the registration fee enables the charity to recover this VAT in full, so you are better off in VAT terms if you charge VAT on registration fees and then recover VAT on the purchase of places. You will have to be registered for VAT to be able to implement this.

It is unlikely that overseas challenge events will be covered by the fundraising event exemption because they will probably involve more than two nights' accommodation. This also applies to UK-based events where more than two nights accommodation is provided. You first need to establish whether the charity is actually organising the event, or whether it is acting as agent for someone else. If the charity *is* organising the event, then it may not be 'in business' – this depends on whether the charity regularly organises such events.

If a challenge event does not qualify as a fundraising event, and it is more than a one-off, you need to consider whether it comes within the Tour Operator's Margin Scheme (TOMS). As trading, these events should probably go through a trading subsidiary. This is not necessarily a financial problem, as the event may still qualify as zero-rated. However, if the event does come within TOMS, the operational rules are different and you need to get this right. There are also a number of rules concerning travel arrangements, which charities need to be aware of, such as ATOL bonding. (More information on these aspects is given in the Institute of Fundraising's *Code of Fundraising Practice* – see *Sources of further information*.)

VAT RECOVERY

Only businesses registered for VAT can recover VAT on purchases. For ordinary businesses and, usually, charities' trading subsidiaries, this is straightforward and all input VAT is recovered. It is frequently not so simple for charities, as they have income that falls into several VAT categories. Most charities will have some donations or grants. Since these are non-business supplies, the recovery of VAT on purchases will be restricted.

Calculating recoverable VAT

The first step is to relate purchases directly to the different areas of activity. This gives the amount of VAT on purchases directly attributable to each category of VAT. The VAT on purchases which cannot be directly related to a particular area of activity, such as shared premises and administration costs, is known as *non-attributable* VAT or residual VAT. Under the standard method, a proportion of this input VAT will be recoverable, depending on the relative amount of taxable business income, compared with the total income. Special methods can be agreed with the VAT office, using a different basis to calculate the proportion of non-attributable VAT to be recovered. The VAT office will consider any basis that will give a fair proportion and which can be checked by their officers. Options might include staff time spent on different activities or the amount of floor space taken up by different activities. You must have the agreement of the VAT office before you start to use a special method.

Whether you use a special method or the standard method, you will need to recalculate your VAT recovery at the end of the tax year to work out any annual adjustment necessary. For this purpose the tax year ends on 31 March, 30 April or 31 May, depending on your VAT quarters.

Partial exemption rules

The partial exemption rules may apply if the charity makes any exempt supplies as well as taxable supplies. (Note that if the charity makes only exempt supplies or only exempt and non-business supplies then it will not be allowed to register for VAT and therefore will not be able to recover any VAT.) The *de minimis* limits allow charities with low amounts of input VAT attributable to exempt activity to recover this VAT. The *de minimis* limit is £625 per month on average and not more than 50 per cent of total input VAT. The percentage test is to ensure that the exempt activity is a minor part of the organisation's total activity. Note that the term 'input tax' means the VAT on *business* purchases in VAT law, so the VAT on purchases relating to non-business activity is not strictly input VAT. Therefore, when undertaking the partial exemption calculations, the 50 per cent test should be applied to business input VAT only.

Organisations with exempt activity need to check the *de minimis* limit every time they prepare a VAT return and they also have to undertake an annual adjustment. This means a recalculation of the figures on an annual basis, to deal with any distortions produced by seasonal variations.

Improving VAT recovery

The options available for individual charities will vary enormously, as they will depend on the nature of the activities and their balance between different categories of VAT. There are a few general rules to consider:

- Identify purchases with particular activities as far as possible. VAT on purchases relating to taxable activities will be 100 per cent recoverable.

- Make use of the partial exemption *de minimis* rule if possible. Remember that fundraising events are exempt even when organised through the trading subsidiary. Both the charity and the trading subsidiary can maximise benefit from these rules if you can stay within the partial exemption *de minimis* limits.

- Increase the proportion of business activities, so that the formula for calculating recoverable VAT on the non-attributable input VAT is more favourable.

- Use a *special method*, which should be agreed with HMRC in advance, for calculating the recovery rate on non-attributable VAT.

- Maximise zero-rated, rather than non-business supplies, e.g. subscriptions where the benefits to members are printed matter can be counted as zero-rated, by agreement with the VAT office. Zero-rated income allows you to recover the related input VAT and increases the taxable proportion of total income, thus improving the proportion of non-attributable VAT to recover. Charity shops selling donated goods should be kept within the charity for this reason, unless you have a group registration.

- If the charity has a trading subsidiary consider group registration. This will mean that the total supplies of the whole group are the basis of the apportionment for calculating the recoverable part of non-attributable input VAT. If the trading subsidiary has significant taxable supplies, the recovery rate will be greatly enhanced.

ZERO-RATING RELIEFS

There is quite a long list of items that are zero-rated for VAT when supplied to a charity, although most are for medical supplies and aids for disabled people. To obtain the zero-rating, the charity has to supply a certificate to the supplier, stating that the purchase qualifies for zero-rating. An example of the certificate is given in the relevant VAT leaflet, which is essential reading for charities working in the medical or disability field. This is a valuable relief to charities, since it is a direct cost saving and available to both VAT registered and unregistered charities.

Examples of the items that should qualify for zero-rating when purchased by a charity include:

- building work to give access to charity-run buildings for disabled people

- special adaptation of toilets and bathrooms for disabled people

- charity advertising (see below)

- specially adapted equipment for use by a disabled person

- ambulances

- lifeboats and rescue equipment

- minibuses for transporting disabled people when purchased by a charity which provides care for them

- talking books for blind people

- medical equipment if purchased out of donated funds.

The conditions for the zero-rating are quite specific and must be adhered to carefully. The onus is on the charity only to provide a certificate for zero-rating to a supplier when it is appropriate. The charity is potentially liable to make good the VAT in the event of error.

Charity advertising

Charities can buy advertising and closely related services at zero-rate VAT. Initially the scope of this relief was restricted to newspaper advertising and to the actual cost of the advertisement. The zero-rating has since been extended to include advertisements in all media and all preparation work, such as design and artwork. In addition, the advertisement no longer has to be specifically for the purpose of raising money or making known the objects of the charity. The effective date of the changes was 1 April 2000.

In order to zero-rate the invoice, the supplier must be satisfied that it is a supply of advertising to a charity. Where the charity is claiming the zero-rating for goods that are closely related to the design or production of an advertisement, it must give the supplier a declaration that the advertisement is for a relevant purpose. The supplier may need to check their action with its local VAT office, because if it makes a mistake, it will have to account for the VAT.

The zero-rating applies to all types of advertising by charities, including recruitment advertisements, attracting new members, pupils or students, advertising events, raising awareness and fundraising.

All media are allowed, including badges, balloons, banners, carrier bags, cinema, TV and radio advertisements, clothing, flags, Internet advertising (except for adverts on the charity's own website), all types of printed matter including business cards, calendars, car parking tickets, diaries, greetings cards, lottery tickets, posters and stationery.

Zero-rating is not available in the following cases:

- Personally addressed letters and other targeted fundraising activities. Direct marketing and telesales cannot therefore be zero-rated. It may be possible for individual items of the promotional material used to be zero-rated. (See also direct mail.)

- Advertising on the charity's own website, or the creation of the charity's own website, even if the website is being used to raise funds.

- Where the charity prepares its own advertisements in-house.

- Where the supply is not directly to a charity, for example where it is to a trading subsidiary.

- Where the advertisement appears in a charity's own magazine, notice board, calendar or other publication.

Adaptations of a building for use by a disabled person

Certain construction services can be zero-rated to a charity where they are to the benefit of a disabled person. These are as follows:

- The supply of services to constructing a ramp or widening a doorway or passage, which makes access or movement easier for disabled people.

- The supply of services of extending or adapting a bathroom, washroom or lavatory so that it can be used by disabled people in a charity-run residential home or day centre (20 per cent of users must be disabled).

- The supply of services of extending or adapting a washroom or a lavatory (but not a bathroom) on premises such as a church hall, day centre or village hall, used mainly by a charity for charitable purposes, so that it can be used by disabled people.

- The supply of services necessary for the installation of a vertical lift in a building where a charity provides permanent or temporary residence or a day centre for disabled people. (Any preparatory or restoration work required as a consequence of the above will also be zero-rated.)

- The provision of a lift providing residential accommodation or for use as a day centre.

- The supply of an alarm system designed to be operated by a disabled person enabling him or her directly to alert a specified person or control centre.

- The repair and maintenance of an item once fitted or installed under one of the above zero ratings.

Professional fees are not covered by the relief, although a design and building company may make use of the recovery of input tax and a zero-rated supply.

PROPERTY TRANSACTIONS AND VAT

The rules on property transactions are very complex and it is wise to seek professional advice. This may prove worthwhile, as the sums involved may be significant.

As a general rule, VAT will always be charged on building repairs, extensions, improvements, refurbishment and alterations. Only new construction of separate buildings may be zero-rated if they will be used for residential purposes or by a charity for its non-business activity. Substantial alterations (those requiring approval) to listed buildings may also qualify for zero-rating, providing the building will be used for non-business purposes by a charity.

If you are planning extensive building works, it is worth considering your VAT position as a whole. The VAT on building costs is recoverable by businesses, unless a large proportion of their income is exempt.

Renting property

Rent will generally be exempt for VAT purposes and must always be exempt for dwellings, buildings for a relevant residential purpose and buildings for a relevant charitable purpose.

Landlords may opt to tax the rent on buildings for commercial and office use. The rent will then be standard-rated.

VAT PLANNING

There is some scope for planning activities to be advantageous from a VAT point of view. The scope is somewhat limited, however, as in some matters you have no choice. Care is needed and professional advice should be obtained. The penalties for misdemeanours and even errors are quite severe.

Avoiding registration

Remember, a whole organisation has to register for VAT, although a separate trading company is a separate legal entity and is therefore registered for VAT in its own right if necessary. You must look at all activities of an entity to check whether the threshold is exceeded. If you channel certain trading activities into the trading company, then it may be possible to keep the charity below the threshold or entirely outside the scope. Consider the following options:

- raise donations rather than sponsorships

- ask for donations rather than charge for entrance

- keep subscriptions largely outside the scope

- fundraise through fundraising events

- obtain sponsorship for fundraising events rather than for regular activities, so that it is included in the exemption.

You may apply for exemption from registration if the majority of your taxable supplies are zero-rated. In order to be exempt from registration, you need to be able to show that you would also be in a repayment situation. In other words, you would always be entitled to recover more VAT than you would be liable to pay over.

Achieving registration

In order to register for VAT, you must have some taxable supplies. You cannot even register voluntarily if you only have non-business and exempt income. Consider:

- charging for entrance to exhibitions, events etc.

- charging for publications (zero-rated)

- providing benefits to members in return for their subscription

- changing fundraising events into regular events

- charging a fee to companies for sponsorship or advertising

- charging the trading company for services.

169

Be careful that you do not end up *trading* in the charity so that a tax liability is incurred. Regular fundraising events and commercial sponsorship would be trading and unlikely to be 'primary purpose' trading, so would potentially be taxable. (The *profits* would be taxable, so if you did find yourself in this predicament, you would identify costs relating to the income as far as possible to reduce the taxable profits.)

Minimising VAT

This is worth consideration by VAT registered and unregistered organisations alike.

- Use zero-rating reliefs as much as possible.

- Buy from other charities or suppliers not registered for VAT.

- Obtain printed matter at zero rates and ensure that all associated work is handled through the printer so that the whole supply is zero-rated.

- Plan building works carefully and obtain at zero rates if possible.

- Use venues run by educational charities for training and conferences as they will be able to exempt the charge.

SUMMARY

VAT legislation is complex and subject to regular change and amendment as new cases go to court and European legislation affects UK law. Care needs to be taken in this area and proper advice sought from a specialist. This chapter is brief and does not cover all aspects in detail, so look at the reference materials for further information if you consider that a particular aspect may apply to your organisation. If you are uncertain about the status of a particular activity or your VAT position, then it is wise to obtain a ruling from your local VAT office. Further changes are anticipated to VAT as it affects charities, since the review announced by the government in the 1997 July Budget. These will be subject to consultation before being introduced, but you should be aware of the changes and the effect these will have on your particular organisation.

11 Tax-effective giving

Charities can benefit from their tax-exempt status to receive donations gross of tax or to reclaim tax that has been paid on the money donated. The range of tax reliefs on charitable giving has been expanded over recent years, so this is now a considerable help to charities receiving voluntary income from individuals and companies.

The main forms of charitable giving that are eligible for tax relief are:

- gift aid
- payroll giving
- gifts of shares and property
- gifts in kind.

Note that the government department dealing with all questions and claims in relation to tax-effective giving is a specialist unit within HM Revenue & Customs (HMRC), referred to as HMRC Charities. Contact details are included in *Sources of further information*.

GIFT AID

This is the principal method by which charities encourage donors to make their donations tax-effective. Since April 2000, gift aid can apply to any amount and can apply to regular giving as well as one-off donations. It is also available to community amateur sports clubs providing they comply with the rules and register with HMRC.

When an individual gives money to charity under gift aid, the charity can reclaim the amount equivalent to the basic rate of tax. So, currently, an individual donating £100 to a charity under gift aid allows the charity to reclaim £28.31. This is because the £100 is net of tax and the basic rate of tax is 22 per cent. The calculation is:

$$£100 \times \frac{22}{78} = £28.21$$

In addition, a higher rate taxpayer can claim higher rate tax relief on their tax return. The donor claims tax relief of (40% − 22%) on the gross donation = 18% × (£100 + £28.21) = £23.08. Therefore the net cost to the donor is £100 − £23.08 = £76.92.

Gift aid can only apply to cash donations and it should not be used for the purchase of goods or services. For example, the purchase of raffle tickets or tickets to fundraising events will not come within gift aid. Certain rules apply to the level of benefit donors may receive whilst still giving under gift aid (see below).

Gifts of foreign currency notes and coins to charities are eligible for gift aid. Guidance from HMRC has confirmed that gift aid can be claimed in the same way as any other donation. You need to keep records of the amounts donated in each currency and calculate the sterling value on the date of the donation.

Company donations

Companies pay donations to charities gross, including them on their corporation tax return to obtain tax relief. Therefore charities do not claim back any tax on company donations. The rules on benefits apply to all companies since April 2006, including public companies. Companies may not use a gift aid donation to purchase goods or services from a charity.

Deeds of covenant

Since April 2000, tax relief for donations under deeds of covenant have come within the gift aid scheme and there is no separate relief for these donations. This means that gift aid forms have to be used and the same conditions apply.

Gift aid for individuals

Only UK taxpayers may make donations under gift aid, but the tax paid may be income tax or capital gains tax. Even though the charity may reclaim tax at the basic rate, it is sufficient if the individual has at least paid tax at the lower rate. Members of the armed forces and government serving overseas and non-resident UK taxpayers may make donations under gift aid. Charities are encouraged to remind regular donors to inform the charity if their tax status changes.

Individuals may claim relief from higher rate tax by entering the gift aid donation on their tax return. The relief given is the difference between basic and higher rates of tax. Since April 2003, taxpayers have been able to carry back the higher rate element of gift aid relief to the previous tax year. In addition, taxpayers will be able to nominate a charity to receive all or part of a tax repayment that is due to them.

Declarations

Individuals have to make a declaration that they wish the charity to treat their donation as gift aid. Gift aid declarations can be given in writing or orally. This includes electronic communications such as use of the Internet, e-mail, fax, telephone, mobile phone or text message. A declaration may be given before or after the donation, and may cover a single donation, a series of donations or all donations from that individual. Declarations should cover the following;

- the name and home address of the donor

- the name of the charity

- a description of the donation(s) to which the declaration relates

- a declaration that the donation(s) is/are to be treated as gift aid donations.

Written declarations should also include a note explaining that the donation must come out of income on which tax has been paid.

Example gift aid declaration

Note that this example contains a space for signature and date; these are not required by law, but they may be useful to prove that the individual provided the declaration and are necessary if the donor is declaring that all donations from the date of the declaration will be gift aid donations.

You may add further information for your own purposes, such as a direct debit mandate. You may also simplify the declaration if you are incorporating it into a form that includes only one option and the gift aid will apply only to that donation. A tick box is sufficient as long as the basic information such as the declaration itself and the donor's name and address are included.

NAME OF CHARITY

DONOR DETAILS
Title   First name   Surname
Address
Postcode

DETAILS OF DONATION

I want the charity to treat

*the enclosed donation of £..........

*all donations I make under the direct debit mandate below

*the donations I make on or after the date of this declaration until I notify you otherwise

as gift aid donations

*delete as appropriate

Signature.. Date..............................

Note that:

■ You should be paying income tax or capital gains tax as this declaration means that the charity will be reclaiming the tax you have paid and adding it to the value of your donation.

■ You can claim higher rate tax relief on this donation by entering the amount of the donation on your tax return.

■ You should notify us if your circumstances change and you are no longer a taxpayer. We will no longer reclaim the tax on your donations.

Please notify us if your personal details such as name or address change so that we can update our records.

A declaration can include the name of more than one charity, for example where a joint fundraising event takes place. In such a situation the charities involved need to ensure that the donor is aware how his or her donation is to be split between the charities listed on the declaration, and they each keep records of how the donations have been divided between them. Each charity will also need to be able to produce a copy of the declaration, if required. Where a charity changes its name (for example because of a merger) it will not need to obtain a new declaration from a donor so long as it can show beyond doubt that the name of the charity on the existing declaration is a name previously used by the charity.

Donors are entitled to cancel their declaration at any time. They may do so by notifying the charity in any convenient way. The charity should keep a record of the cancellation of a declaration, including the date of the donor's notification.

A cancellation will normally have effect only in relation to donations received by the charity on or after the date on which the donor notifies the charity of the cancellation, or such later date as the donor may specify in the cancellation. The charity must not reclaim tax in respect of such donations. Any donations received before the date of the donor's notification will still qualify as gift aid donations.

Telephone declarations

Oral declarations can be given, for example over the telephone. In this case, the charity must send a written record of the declaration. This should include the basic information listed above, such as name, address, charity name and declaration that it is a gift aid donation. In addition, the written record should include the note about donations coming out of taxed income. Extra information for the written record is:

- a note explaining the donor's entitlement to cancel the declaration

- the date on which the donor gave the declaration to the charity

- the date on which the charity sent the written record to the donor.

An oral declaration is only valid if the charity has sent a written declaration or has a verifiable audio record of the oral declaration. Donors can cancel their declaration at any time, but with oral declarations they can also cancel the declaration retrospectively if they do so within 30 days from the date the written record was sent.

Written records of oral declarations may be generated and retained by electronic means and can, for example, be sent to the donor by e-mail. The system will need to be set up in such a way that an audit by HMRC will still be able to verify that the written record has been sent to the donor.

Joint declarations and partnerships

It is possible for spouses and people living together to make a joint declaration on the same form (in effect, there are two gift aid declarations). The joint declaration must include the full name and address of each person. Both parties will need to make clear to the charity involved how much of any donation relates to each of them. They will also need this information for their own tax affairs. The charity will need to list each person separately on the R68 Gift Aid schedule form that accompanies its claim and show the donation received from each.

In England, Wales and Northern Ireland a business partnership does not have a legal personality. So, a donation by a partnership is treated as having been made by the underlying partners. One partner may make a gift aid declaration on behalf of all the partners, provided he or she has the power to do so under the terms of the partnership agreement or some other instrument given under seal. In that case it will be sufficient for the declaration to show the name and address of the partnership. Otherwise, it will be necessary for each partner to make his or her own gift aid declaration. They may do so on the same declaration form, provided it lists all their names and home addresses.

Limited liability partnerships and partnerships in Scotland have a legal personality. So, in all cases, one of the partners may make a gift aid declaration on behalf of the partnership, showing the name and address of the partnership.

The partners should enter their share of the donation on their own self-assessment return. How the donation is apportioned between the partners is a matter for them to decide.

Benefits rules on gift aid

Some benefits are allowed despite the general rule that the donation should be a pure gift. There is a sliding scale of allowable benefit, depending on the level of donation.

Total donations in the tax year	Total value of benefits allowed in the tax year
£0–£100	25%
£101–£1,000	£25
£1,001 +	5%

The absolute maximum value of benefits in a tax year is £500. These limits apply separately to each donation, but you also have to review the total amount received from a donor over a whole tax year. It is therefore possible that you will have treated gifts received early in the year as gift aid donations, but that the accumulation of donations and benefits leads to the elimination of donations from that individual or company from gift aid. Note that the benefit rules apply to both companies and individuals.

Benefits provided to a member of the donor's family will also be caught under these rules, as they may be a 'connected person'. A person is connected with the donor if that person is

- the wife or husband

- a relative (e.g. brother, sister), ancestor (e.g. mother) or lineal descendant (e.g. grandson)

- the wife or husband of a relative

- a company under the control of the donor, or under the control of connected persons.

A benefit is any item or service provided by the charity or a third party to the donor or a person connected with the donor, in consequence of making the donation.

If the benefits exceed the limits, the donation cannot qualify under the gift aid scheme.

Additional rules for companies (applying to all companies since 1 April 2006) are:

- the donation may not be made subject to a condition as to repayment

- the donation may not be conditional on, or part of arrangements for, the charity's acquisition of property from the company or a connected person, otherwise than by way of gift.

Membership subscriptions

Membership subscriptions may be donated under gift aid, providing the benefits provided under the membership scheme fall within the limits listed above. HMRC disregards annual reports, newsletters, magazines, members' handbooks and programmes of events providing further information about the charity's work when considering what constitutes a benefit. Free admission to events or reduced prices count as benefits and need to be valued.

Sometimes charities secure discounts for their members from outside suppliers. These discounts will count as benefits if they are received as a result of the membership subscription.

The rules for gift aid are not the same as those for VAT, and it is possible that a charity would have to calculate an apportionment of benefits for VAT purposes, even though they are benefits that are allowed or disregarded for gift aid purposes.

Valuation of benefits

A mere acknowledgement will not count as a benefit and does not need to be valued. Companies making donations to charity under gift aid may not receive free promotion or advertising as a result of their donation so, for example, this precludes the prominent display of their logo on a charity's literature or website.

The usual basis for valuing a benefit is to look for the price that would be paid in a commercial setting by a third party. This may be the cover price on a magazine or book, or the normal ticket price for an event. Where there is no comparison with the commercial value of the goods or service, the charity has to assess the value to the recipient. It may be necessary to calculate the benefit by reference to the cost to the charity where there is no external comparison. For example, a charity should calculate cost per head for an event that is not open to the public.

Information about the charity's work contained in newsletters, bulletins, magazines and journals will be accepted as having nil value under these rules. This will be the case even if the publication has a cover price. Note that the information has to be relevant to the charity's objects and educate readers or promote the work of the charity.

Where the benefit is a discount or a reduced price, it may be difficult to calculate the value to the donor because the level of take-up will determine the total value of the benefit. In these circumstances, HMRC will accept a calculation based on the overall level of take-up to assess the value of the discount.

Example

As a membership benefit, members may attend training courses organised by the charity at half price. New members attend far more courses and take advantage of the discount to a greater extent than members of several years' standing. The total value of the benefit to all members in a year can be ascertained from the record of attendance at training courses. The total value of benefits is then divided by the total number of members to calculate the value of this benefit per member.

Care is needed when benefits such as discounts may be spread over less than 12 months, as there may then be a need to annualise the benefit and the donation received.

Example

A single payment of £100 to a theatre gives the donor the right to a 10 per cent discount on theatre tickets purchased in the next six months, valued at £24. On the face of it, this is within the benefit limits set out in the table above. However, annualising applies to both the donation and the benefit because the benefits are for a period of less than 12 months. So their annual value is double these amounts for the purpose of checking the benefit limits. Thus the annualised figures are £200 for the donation and £48 for the benefits. Thus, the value of the benefits exceeds £25 and gift aid may not apply. Had the scheme been amended so that the period for the discount was one year, then annualising would not apply.

Splitting benefits

Where the value of benefits would exceed the limits in the donor benefit rules, the donor may specify that part of his or her payment is to be treated as payment for the benefits and part is to be treated as a donation.

This treatment can only apply where:

- the item has a readily ascertainable value, for example the benefit can be purchased separately

- the excess is clearly given with the purpose of donating to the charity

- the donor is aware of the value of the benefit at the time he or she makes the donation.

Provided the donor specifies this before, or at the time of, making the donation, the part of the payment that is specified as a donation may qualify as a gift aid donation. The charity and donor should keep evidence of how the payment was to be split – a copy of a dated letter accompanying the payment, for example. Alternatively, separate payments could be made.

Admission charges to heritage or conservation sites

Up until April 2006, only charities that had the preservation of heritage property or the conservation of wildlife as their sole or main purpose could disregard a right of admission given in return for a donation in determining whether the benefits received by a donor, or connected person, exceeded those allowed. There was no restriction on the level of donation that could benefit from the exemption.

New rules introduced from 6 April 2006 broaden the scope of the exemption so that all charities where the public pays an admission charge to view qualifying property can benefit from the exemption. This includes museums, zoos, art galleries, gardens and other visitor centres. The new rules will apply where the following conditions are met.

Either

- The visitor makes a donation that is at least 10 per cent more than the admission charge for the equivalent right of admission.

Or

The donation secures admission to the property for a 12-month period, for example through a season ticket or a membership scheme. Access should in general be unlimited whenever the property is open to the public during that 12-month period, but charities may exclude from the right of admission up to five days in each 12-month period when the property is otherwise open to the public and still qualify.

Example

A charity maintains a garden, which it opens to the public for three months each year, charging a daily admission fee. Once a month during this season, open-air concerts are held in the garden for which a higher admission fee is charged. The charity runs a friends scheme whereby those donating above a certain amount are allowed free access to the garden whenever it is open to the public except on concert days. This scheme qualifies under the gift aid rules.

Any charity that makes a charge to the public for viewing property may seek gift aid donations if the criteria are met. The legislation lists the following types of property that will qualify as long as they are property that is preserved, maintained, kept or created by a charity as part of furthering its charitable objects:

- buildings

- artefacts

- plants

- animals

- grounds or other land

- property of a scientific nature

- works of art (but not performances).

This list is illustrative and not intended to be exhaustive. For example, it is accepted that interactive experiments with an educational purpose and displays of military memorabilia will also qualify. Although the price of tickets purchased for performances, for example plays and concerts, cannot attract gift aid, visits to view theatrical establishments or concert venues will qualify if the criteria are met.

Some charities offer family tickets. Where a family ticket admits the purchaser and members of their family and the ticket meets the conditions, the donor who purchases the family ticket may complete a gift aid declaration for the whole sum paid, thus enabling the charity to reclaim the tax repayment. The definition of 'family' is a matter for the charity to decide in accordance with its admissions policy. It is likely that the charity will decide to set limits on the number of adults and/or children who can be admitted by a family ticket. There is no expectation that the charity will make identity or relationship checks on individuals admitted by a family ticket. It is not necessary for all individuals included in the family ticket to enter together. Gift aid is limited to tickets admitting the purchaser and their family; it does not extend to *any* group ticket.

Charities that open to the public free of charge but seek voluntary donations from visitors are not subject to this legislation. Gift aid may be claimed on any genuinely voluntary donation made, as long as the charity and the donor comply with the benefits rules.

These rules on donations and admissions mean that the value of the admission is not taken into account when considering what benefits have been given to the donor in return for the donation. If charities wish to provide additional modest benefits they may do so, provided the value of those benefits does not exceed the standard gift aid benefit limits.

CHARITY AUCTIONS An entire auction payment will only qualify as a gift aid payment if the normal requirements of the gift aid scheme are met, which includes satisfying the gift aid benefit rules.

The 'benefit' of a charity auction item is:

■ For an item that is commercially available, the benefit for gift aid purposes is its 'shop sale' price. An item must have a clear and recognisable value (market value) and be available for purchase separately by an individual.

■ For a commercially available item that has had its value enhanced, for example because it has been owned by a celebrity, the market value (and hence the benefit for gift aid purposes) will be the amount it fetches in the auction, not its original price.

■ For an item not commercially available, its value is the auction price paid by the purchaser. So the benefit for gift aid purposes is the auction price paid.

Where the value of the benefits exceeds the limits in the donor benefit rules, the donor can treat part of their payment as buying the benefits and part (the excess) as a donation. This treatment only applies where the item is commercially available and the donor is aware at the time they make a successful bid that the item could be purchased separately and for what price. The successful bidder must still complete a gift aid declaration covering the donation element of the bid price. As this would normally be completed after the auction of the item, this cannot then provide evidence that the bidder was aware of the availability and value of the item at the time of making their bid. Examples of such evidence include details provided in an auction catalogue.

Sponsored events

Donations raised through sponsorship of individuals in an event are donations from the third party to the charity. It is not valid for the individual participant to collect the cash from sponsors and then make one gift aid donation of that money to the charity. However, it is possible to collect gift aid declarations from the individual sponsors. This can be achieved on one form that is both a sponsorship form and a declaration. The suggested format is for the gift aid declaration for a one-off donation to be printed at the top of the sponsorship sheet, with individual donors able to opt in by ticking a box. The information gathered on the form must include the sponsor's name and home address, including postcode, and the amount actually collected. It may be necessary to record the date collected and the date the money is actually handed over to the charity. It has to be possible to trace the amounts entered in the charity's own books back to individual donors and their declarations.

Care is needed with the benefits rules in relation to these events. Donations from connected persons may not be eligible for gift aid if the participant is receiving benefits as a result of taking part in the event. One way of checking this would be to add a tick box to ask if the person is connected to the participant.

Entry fees or participation fees paid by the participant are not eligible for gift aid; they are not gifts. If the participant part-pays a participation fee this reduces the value of the benefit by the amount paid. If the participant pays the full participation fee the benefit is reduced to nil and donations by the participant and connected persons qualify for gift aid.

VOLUNTEERS' EXPENSES Voluntary workers sometimes incur expenditure when assisting charities to carry out their work (for example, travel costs, postal or photo-copying charges). Provided the expenses are reasonable and proper, a charity can reimburse a volunteer. Often a volunteer will forgo the expenses to which they are entitled. The forgone expenses can be gift aided but only if the charity physically pays the expenses to the volunteer. The volunteer is then free to keep the money or pay part or all of it back to the charity as a gift aid payment. If they give all the expenses back to the charity, they are not returning the expenses but making a payment of an equivalent amount.

A gift aid payment to a charity cannot be made by book entries following a waiver of expenses.

GIFTS OF GOODS AND SERVICES Gift aid only applies to gifts of money. If a supporter gives something other than money, gift aid will not be available if ownership of the asset passes to the charity. However, if the charity or its subsidiary trading company agrees with the supporter to sell the item on the supporter's behalf, the supporter can then give the proceeds to the charity, which can claim gift aid. This can apply to the sale of donated goods in charity shops, and some charities have initiated schemes to enable them to recover gift aid in this way. The charity or its subsidiary is acting as an agent on behalf of the supporter to sell the item, which remains the possession of the supporter until it is sold. When it is sold the charity must inform the supporter of the sale price. Since a donation must be voluntary in order to qualify for gift aid, a mechanism needs to be in place to ensure the donation is voluntary.

In practice it is likely that charities wishing to arrange sales on behalf of supporters will have a written agreement with the supporter which:

- establishes the charity or its subsidiary as an agent to sell the items on behalf of the supporter

- itemises the goods to be sold

- obtains a gift aid declaration from the supporter

- informs the supporter of the nature of the scheme and that they have the option of claiming the cash when they are notified of the sale price.

As selling goods on behalf of others is a non-charitable trading activity (assuming it is not one-off) this would jeopardise the charitable tax exemptions and if undertaken on any scale should be managed through a trading subsidiary. For VAT purposes the sale of donated goods by a charity (or by a trading subsidiary that donates its profits to the charity) is zero-rated. Supplying a sale of agency services is a different activity and so this needs to be considered as well as the gift aid issues.

The individual needs to have the opportunity to change their mind about giving and to receive all or part of the proceeds. This ensures that the payment is an entirely voluntary gift. It also protects the donor from giving more than intended in the event of the asset selling for far more than expected and protects the charity from any allegations of inappropriate practice.

HMRC prefers arrangements under which the individual is asked to confirm that they wish to go ahead and donate the sale proceeds to the charity. However, it is acceptable for the charity to provide sale details to the donor and explain that it will act in accordance with the individual's earlier instructions and treat sales proceeds as a gift to the charity identified unless the individual advises it otherwise within a specified period. To allow for postal delays and absences due to holidays etc. HMRC would not expect periods of less than 21 days to be specified. Charities will need to consider how they will handle requests from individuals to take the proceeds after the specified period has expired, and make their position clear in any guidance and documentation for staff and donors.

The charity can make gift aid repayment claims in the normal way; no special arrangements are required. The claim can be made as soon as the charity receives confirmation from the donor that they wish to go ahead and donate the sale proceeds as notified to the charity (or the 21-day period mentioned above has elapsed). The charity will need to retain all documentation associated with the sale for audit purposes. In addition to retaining the gift aid declaration, the charity will also need to be able to produce any agreement with the individual under which it or its subsidiary is appointed the donor's agent to sell the item. Documentation confirming the sale proceeds and confirming that the donor has been notified and had the opportunity to receive all or part of the proceeds rather than donating them should also be retained. Normal gift aid requirements to provide an audit trail will also apply.

Some charities may want to use sites such as eBay to sell the assets on behalf of the individual, who then donates the proceeds to the charity. In such arrangements the commercial operator may charge a commission, which is deducted from the sale proceeds. As long as the individual is under no obligation to give the proceeds to the charity, gift aid will be available on any amounts that they give. The commercial operator will almost certainly be VAT registered and so will have to charge VAT on the commission.

Transactions with substantial donors

Charities will be treated as having incurred non-qualifying expenditure, causing a restriction of tax relief on an equal amount of income or gains as above, where they enter into certain transactions with substantial donors. The new rules were introduced in the Finance Act 2006 and affect transactions taking place on or after 22 March 2006.

The Treasury states 'the new rules are targeted at charities controlled by a donor, where the charity is used as a personal moneybox and the actions of the charity and donor are in effect the same. It is not possible to delineate donor-controlled charities in a way that is not easily circumvented and the clause will instead target behaviours that carry risk.'

A substantial donor is a person or a company who gives:

- £25,000 or more in any 12-month period, or

- £100,000 or more over a six-year period.

They will be substantial donors for the period in which the limits are exceeded and the following five chargeable periods. This means that someone may now be a substantial donor in respect of donations made before the effective date and that someone may become a substantial donor affecting transactions that occurred before they qualified as a substantial donor.

The substantial donor rules extend to people connected with the substantial donor. So if an affected transaction takes place between the charity and the wife, partner, sibling, lineal ancestor or descendant, connected company or business partner of the substantial donor, the transaction is also caught.

The donation may be in money or money's worth and includes donated assets, facilities, services etc. valued at market value.

The following transactions are affected:

The sale or letting of property by a charity to a substantial donor.

The sale or letting of property to a charity by a substantial donor.

The provision of services by a charity to a substantial donor.

The provision of services to a charity by a substantial donor.

An exchange of property between a charity and a substantial donor.

The provision of financial assistance by a charity to a substantial donor.

The provision of financial assistance to a charity by a substantial donor.

Investment by a charity in the business of a substantial donor, unless listed on a recognised stock exchange.

Payment of remuneration by the charity to the substantial donor unless an approved payment to a trustee.

The following transactions are excluded:

Transactions with wholly owned subsidiaries.

Transactions with connected registered social landlords (RSLs). A charity and an RSL are connected if one is wholly owned or controlled by the other or both are wholly owned or controlled by the same person.

Supplies of property or services by the donor will not be affected where they are made in the course of the donor's business, and not for the avoidance of tax. The terms must be no less beneficial to the charity than could be obtained from an arm's length transaction.

Supplies of services by the charity to the donor where these are primary purpose supplies and on terms no more beneficial to the donor than could be obtained from an arm's length transaction.

Financial assistance by a donor, on terms no more beneficial to the donor than could be obtained from an arm's length transaction.

Where a transaction is caught:

Any payment by the charity will be considered non-qualifying expenditure, leading to restriction of tax relief on the basis described above.

Where a payment is made by the donor that is not on arm's-length terms, the difference between the payment and arm's-length terms, to the extent that this benefits the donor, will be treated as non-qualifying expenditure by the charity. HMRC will make the determination of the difference.

Record keeping

The gift aid rules require the retention of all written declarations received and copies of the written records sent to donors who have made a telephone declaration. You need to be able to link the declaration to the donations made by that particular donor. Charities will therefore need to think through a system that will achieve this, perhaps using reference numbers. It also means that declarations made for all future donations will need to be kept for a very long time. You may need to consider whether you will have a system of refreshing these on a regular basis.

Examples of what is likely to be considered an acceptable record of declarations include:

Written declarations made by the donor or a ticked box confirmation by the donor that they wish gift aid to apply to the donation.

A recording of the making of a declaration by the donor or a recording of the donor confirming a declaration where the declaration is pre-recorded by the charity.

A computer record of a declaration template filled in by the donor and containing a link to the donor's banking details.

An e-mailed copy of a declaration.

A computer 'screen print' of the declaration sent to the charity.

A scanned image of a declaration.

A copy of a mobile phone text message confirmation of a declaration.

There must be a clear link back to the donor, so, for example, the transcribing of declaration details given by donors into a database will not satisfy the requirements.

Records must be kept:

- For charitable companies: for six years after the end of the accounting period to which the tax reclaim relates, though for donations in perpetuity records must be kept until six years after the end of the accounting period in which the last donation is received (i.e. the donor has died).

- For unincorporated charities the later of 31 January next but one after the end of the tax year to which the tax reclaim relates and one year after you make your tax reclaim, rounded to the end of the next quarter.

Claims

Claims for repayment of income tax have to be submitted to HMRC on form R68 and accompanying schedules. In particular, charities must complete the supplementary pages where the details of all gift aid donations have to be listed. There is a substitute schedule available for claims relating to gift aid arising from sponsored events. HMRC also recommends that a separate claim be made for this type of gift aid to make the claim more straightforward. If it is a very large event, then prior notice should be given to HMRC.

Before making their first claim, charities need to register with HMRC, and may be asked to submit their governing instrument and last audited accounts to validate their entitlement to reclaim tax on donations. Claims may then be made as frequently as the charity wishes. Claims should relate to only one tax year, however. Charities may substitute their own forms, but this should be agreed with HMRC in advance. This may be appropriate for charities using computer software to generate claims.

Charities will only be reclaiming tax paid by individuals, as companies no longer deduct tax from gift aid donations to charities.

Claims may also include income tax deducted at source from interest on bank and building society accounts (if not receiving this gross), royalties and other types of annual payment.

Gift aid audits

HMRC undertakes regular audits of charities making substantial gift aid claims. In particular, it is looking for declarations to support the gift aid claims for individuals. It will attempt to trace an amount shown on a gift aid claim to the cash records, bank statements and the individual donor record showing the declaration. If an amount has been improperly claimed, then this has to be paid back to HMRC.

HMRC will check:

■ That a valid gift aid declaration is held for every donation on which gift aid is claimed. The charity has to hold these in such a way that they can be traced back from the gift aid claim.

■ That the actual amount of cash has been received. It will want to trace gift aid claims back to cash books or equivalent records.

■ That the benefit rules have not been breached. This includes donations from connected persons on participatory events.

■ That the gift aid claim has been accurately prepared.

Charities should be aware that during gift aid audits HMRC staff will also be on the look out for non-compliance with PAYE regulations, breach of the conditions for charitable tax reliefs (for example, significant levels of non-primary purpose trading or non-charitable expenditure) and VAT problems. If discovered, other HMRC departments will be notified and further visits may be expected.

If the number of individual claims is large, HMRC states that it will test the claims by selecting a representative sample on a random basis, stratifying where appropriate. If it finds errors in the sample, it will extrapolate that rate of error to the whole of the charity's gift aid claims. So, if, for example, HMRC finds that gift aid to the value of £500 has been claimed when it should not have been, out of a test sample of £10,000, it will assume an error rate of 5 per cent across the whole of the gift aid claims. This is taken back to the last inspection or the previous six years. It will ask the charity to repay 5 per cent of all gift aid claims made during that time.

The charity may ask for further time to produce paperwork or prove that the error rate should not be applied across the whole of its claims, but the onus is on the charity to prove that the error rate does not apply. It should be noted that if different sets of gift aid donations were subject to different processes such that the error rate is likely to vary across the claims, the statistical validity of selecting a random sample from the entire population without stratification is open to challenge. HMRC's approach of backdating assessments on claims may be similarly challenged if it can be shown that the process or processes leading to the errors identified did not exist or were not as significant in the past. It is a good idea to establish the boundaries between different forms of donations in advance. HMRC will ask for background information at the time it arranges the visit. It is appropriate to say at this point that you operate different procedures for different types of donations. It also helps if you keep claims for each type of donation separate. So, for example, you may handle a claim for gift aid on an event separately from the gift aid on regular giving.

It is usually straightforward to establish an audit trail for donations received by cheque, debit card or credit card. However, there can be difficulties in linking cash donations to gift aid declarations and tracking that donation from the time it is made to the time it is banked by the charity. HMRC's main concern is that a pool of cash collected on an unattributable basis is arbitrarily allocated to individuals for whom a gift aid declaration is held and claims made on that basis. There are other risks with cash collections that need to be addressed:

Individuals do not complete the gift aid declarations properly. Many cash collections will take place in hurried situations or even without the presence of charity personnel.

Individuals enter a different amount on the declaration to the amount actually donated. Discrepancies between cash received and declaration totals may cause problems at a gift aid audit and jeopardise the whole collection.

HMRC's recommended way of handling cash donations is:

The individual seals a cash donation in an envelope with a pre-printed gift aid declaration on the outside. The individual completes the declaration if desired and enters the amount of the donation on the outside of the envelope.

The envelopes are opened in the presence of a charity official with the amount contained in each being checked against the statement on the outside and attributed to the named individual on a list; if a valid gift aid declaration has been completed the entry is marked as such on the list.

■ The list is reviewed for other individuals who have not made declarations on the envelope but for whom the charity holds a relevant declaration and the list is amended accordingly.

The list is linked to the relevant banking and a two-way audit trail is created.

The envelopes that include the gift aid declarations are incorporated into the system for storing gift aid declarations and retained for the relevant period

Where a charity has not maintained an auditable record of gift aid declarations, or where HMRC believes that the records are insufficient to show that the donor made the declaration, it may be possible to validate declarations by sending a written statement to the donor – this includes a statement sent by e-mail. The written statement should contain:

all the information provided by the donor in their declaration

an explanation that the donor must have paid enough income tax or capital gains tax to cover that reclaimed by the charity

the date on which the charity sent the written statement to the donor

a statement giving the donor 30 days from the date of the written statement in which to cancel the gift aid declaration.

HMRC will accept that a written confirmation has been issued where the charity can show a standard letter template in an acceptable format and a list of the donors to which the letter was sent. Where the donor cancels their declaration within 30 days, the declaration will be treated as if it was never made. The charity must maintain an auditable record of all written statements and cancellation notices. If the written statement is marked 'returned to sender' or 'not known at this address' the charity should treat the declaration as if it had been cancelled and it must keep a record of the cancellation.

If the donor does not cancel the declaration then it will be treated as valid and gift aid can be reclaimed by the charity on the gift or gifts to which it applies. The charity must maintain records of the written statements and any cancellation notices to a suitable standard to enable the records to be audited.

PAYROLL GIVING

Individuals may give to a nominated charity by direct deduction from their pay. This can apply to pensioners as well as those in employment. The scheme has to be operated by the employer, who deducts the donation from gross pay before calculating the tax due, in a similar way to pension deductions. The employer then sends the amount of the donation to an intermediary or payroll giving agent. Agents are generally consortia of charities and are charities themselves, approved by HMRC. The agent collates the amounts sent from different employers and distributes them to the charities nominated by the employees.

There is no minimum or maximum on the amount that can be given in this way. Donors may not benefit in any way and should receive nothing in return for their donation. They may receive items of nominal value and information about the work of the charity. Agencies must distribute funds to charities within 60 days of receipt from the employer.

Agencies may charge an amount for administration and this is usually deducted from the amount distributed to the charity.

GIFTS OF SHARES

Since April 2000, individuals and companies have been able to get tax relief on shares donated to charities. Qualifying shares and securities are:

- Shares and securities listed or dealt in on the UK stock exchange, including the Alternative Investment Market (AIM).

Shares and securities listed or dealt in on recognised foreign stock exchanges (see list published by HMRC as an appendix to leaflet IR178 and on the HMRC website).

Units in an authorised unit trust.

Shares in an open-ended investment company.

Holdings in certain foreign collective investment schemes.

Where there is any doubt as to whether the shares qualify, then advice should be sought from HMRC.

The amount of relief is calculated as:

the market value of the shares at the date of disposal

plus the transaction costs, such as broker's fees

less any amounts or benefits received from the charity as a result of the gift of shares.

The date of disposal will normally be the date the stock transfer form is signed.

Individuals show this amount as a deduction from taxable income on their tax return. The value of the tax relief is therefore dependent on whether they are a higher rate taxpayer, as relief will be given at the marginal rate of tax. In addition, the individual does not include the disposal of the shares when calculating capital gains for the year. The charity does not reclaim any tax on this form of gift.

Companies may give shares they hold as investments, but not shares in their own company. They may be given or sold at less than market value. Relief is given to companies by allowing the amount as a deduction against company profits for corporation tax purposes. The disposal of the shares is excluded from any chargeable gains calculations.

GIFTS OF PROPERTY TO CHARITIES

Since April 2002, individuals and companies wishing to give property to charities have been able to do so under similar rules to the gift of shares.

GIFTS IN KIND

This principally applies to businesses wishing to support charities, and can include sole traders, partnerships and companies. There are a number of ways in which businesses may wish to give. Gifts in kind do not qualify for gift aid, but instead the business may claim relief by deducting the relevant amount from their taxable profits.

Donated equipment or trading stock must be an article manufactured or sold in the course of the trade, or equipment used in the course of the trade. In this case, no action is needed, but relief is given by a relaxation of the normal rules which require the inclusion of the market value as a deemed disposal. Donated fixed assets should be included in the capital allowances calculation at nil proceeds.

The secondment of an employee to work for a charity on a temporary basis qualifies for relief, which is given by allowing the total employment costs as a tax deductible expense.

Sources of further information

Charity Commission for England and Wales
Charity Commission Direct,
tel: 0845 30000 218
www.charitycommission.gov.uk

HM Revenue & Customs
Charities Helpline, tel: 08453 02 02 03
www.hmrc.gov.uk

Companies House
Contact Centre, Tel: 0870 33 33 636
www.companieshouse.gov.uk

Charity Finance Directors' Group
Tel: 0845 345 3192
www.cfdg.org.uk

Charities' Tax Reform Group
Tel: 020 7222 1265
www.ctrg.org.uk

National Council for Voluntary Organisations (NCVO)
Helpdesk, tel: 0800 2 798 798
www.ncvo-vol.org.uk

Scottish Council for Voluntary Organisations (SCVO)
Information Service, tel: 0800 169 0022
www.scvo.org.uk

Wales Council for Voluntary Action (WCVA)
Tel: 0800 28888 329
www.wcva.org.uk

Northern Ireland Council for Voluntary Action (NICVA)
Tel: 028 9087 7777
www.nicva.org

Institute of Fundraising
Tel: 020 7840 1000
www.institute-of-fundraising.org.uk

The Charity Law Association
Tel: 023 9228 2725
www.charitylawassociation.org.uk

Association of Charitable Foundations
Tel: 020 7255 4499
www.acf.org.uk

National Association for Voluntary and Community Action (NAVCA)
Tel: 0114 278 6636
www.navca.org.uk

acevo (Association of Chief Executives of Voluntary Organisations)
Tel: 0845 345 8481
www.acevo.org.uk

Charities Aid Foundation
Tel: 01732 520 000
www.cafonline.org

Charity Investors' Group
Tel: 020 7658 2480
www.charityinvestorsgroup.org.uk

Office of the Scottish Charity Regulator
Tel: 01382 220446
www.oscr.org.uk

Further reading

Other titles by Kate Sayer in the **Practical Guide** *series, published by the Directory of Social Change in association with Sayer Vincent*

A Practical Guide to Charity Accounting, DSC
A Practical Guide to VAT, DSC

Finance
Funding our Future II: Understand and allocate costs, acevo
The Charity Treasurer's Handbook, Gareth G Morgan, DSC
Financial Stewardship of Charities, Adrian Poffley, DSC
The Charities Manual (Tolley's, published every 3-4 months)

Tax and Trading
Craigmyle Guide to Charitable Giving and Taxation, Craigmyle Co
Tolley's VAT Guide, Tolley
Charities and Taxation, Adrian Randall and Stephen Williams, ICSA

Charity Law
The Voluntary Sector Legal Handbook, Sandy Adirondack and James Sinclair Taylor, DSC
Voluntary but not Amateur, Ruth Hayes and Jacki Reason, LVSC
The Fundraiser's Guide to the Law, Bates, Wells & Braithwaite and Centre for Voluntary Sector Development, DSC, in association with CAF
Data Protection for Voluntary Organisations, Paul Ticher, DSC, in association with Bates, Wells and Braithwaite
Charity Law A-Z: Key Questions Answered, John Claricot & Hilary Philips, Jordans
Charitable Status: A Practical Handbook, Julian Blake with Bates, Wells & Braithwaite

Investment
Investing Charity Funds, Michael Harbottle, Jordans
Managing Charitable Investments, John Harrison, ICSA
The Good Investment Guide for the Voluntary Sector, Catherine Wood, NCVO

Management

Managing without Profit, Mike Hudson, DSC

The Health and Safety Handbook, Al Hinde & Charlie Kavanagh, DSC in association with Health @ Work

Essential Volunteer Management, Steve McCurley & Rick Lynch, DSC

Just about Managing, Sandy Adirondack, LVSC

Managing People, Gill Taylor & Christine Thomton, DSC

Managing Recruitment and Selection, Gill Taylor, DSC

Leadership 101, Brian Rothwell and Margaret Lloyd, DSC

The Pleasure and the Pain: The no-fibbing guide to working with people, Debra Allcock Tyler, DSC

It's Tough at the Top: The no-fibbing guide to leadership, Debra Allcock Tyler, DSC

Databases

Fundraising Databases, Peter Flory, DSC in association with the Institute of Fundraising and CAF

Glossary of common accounting terms

Accruals basis A method of accounting which adjusts the receipts and payments for amounts that should have been collected or paid before the end of the accounting period to arrive at the income and expenditure account.

Assets The money, goods and property an organisation possesses, including any legal rights it may have to receive money, goods, services and property from others.

Balance sheet A summary of the assets and liabilities of an organisation at a particular date. Sometimes described as a 'snapshot' of an organisation. It also describes the funds which are represented by the net assets.

Capital budget The plan for large-scale expenditure on building or equipment, together with the funding plan.

Capital The capital of a charity is a restricted fund (or funds) which the trustees must retain for the benefit of the charity and not spend. A capital fund is known as an endowment fund.

Capitalisation When property or equipment is purchased and treated as an asset on the balance sheet, it is said to be capitalised. This means that the cost is not treated as an operating cost and is not charged to the expense accounts.

Charitable activities This comprises all expenditure relating to the objects of the charity. It includes grants payable, and the cost of supporting charitable activities and projects and governance of the charity.

Cost of generating funds The costs of activities undertaken for a fundraising purpose.

Creditors The amounts owed by an organisation to others; included in liabilities.

Debtors The amounts owed to the organisation for goods or services supplied. 'Aged debtors' is a breakdown of the total owed to the organisation month by month.

Depreciation An allowance for wear and tear made on long-lasting property and equipment. An amount charged annually as an expense to spread the cost of fixed assets over their useful economic life.

Designated funds Unrestricted funds which the trustees have earmarked for a particular purpose.

Endowment A special type of restricted fund that must be retained intact and not spent.

Expendable endowment A type of endowment fund where trustees have the discretion eventually to convert the fund into expendable income.

Financial Reporting Standard A statement of required good practice for all company accounts and all accounts which purport to give a true and fair view. It is obligatory for all published accounts to comply with Financial Reporting Standards. They are issued by a committee of accounting bodies and cover a range of accounting topics, with updated versions issued regularly.

Financial statements The accounts of an organisation including the notes to the accounts and any other statements which need to be included.

Fixed assets Assets that continue to be of value to the organisation year after year and which the trustees hold on a long-term basis and therefore do not intend to dispose of in the short term.

General funds Unrestricted funds that have not been earmarked and may be used generally to further the charity's stated objects.

Impairment The term used to describe a fall in value of an asset. An impairment review may be required for certain tangible fixed assets. This is usually when some major event has occurred which causes you to think that the previous values ascribed to the asset are no longer valid.

Incoming resources All resources available to a charity, including incoming capital (endowment), restricted income, gifts in kind and intangible income.

Liabilities The amounts owed by an organisation at the balance sheet date. The cost will already have been incurred, but the bill has not been paid.

Net book value The net book value is calculated for tangible fixed assets by taking the original cost or valuation amount and deducting the accumulated depreciation. The net book value is the amount at which tangible fixed assets are stated in the balance sheet.

Permanent endowment A type of endowment fund where the trustees must retain the fund intact as capital and use the funds to generate income or hold the assets (depending on the terms of the trust). The trustees have no discretion to convert the endowment into expendable income.

Restricted fund A fund subject to specific trusts within the objects of the charity (e.g. by a letter from the donor at the time of the gift, or by the terms of a public appeal). It may be a capital fund, which cannot be spent but must be retained for the benefit of the charity, or it may be an income fund, which must be spent on the specified purpose within a reasonable time.

Statement of financial activities Abbreviated to SoFA. Financial statement introduced especially for charities in the SORP. Summarises all incoming resources and application of resources. Replacing the income and expenditure account as a primary financial statement, it goes further by bringing together all the transactions of a charity.

Statement of Recommended Practice Guidance on the appropriate treatment of items in the accounts of specialised bodies.

Stock The value of goods on hand at the balance sheet date will be included in stock under current assets.

Support costs These are part of the direct charitable expenditure and may be the management of projects from a central office. They may include a fair proportion of central office running costs.

Tangible fixed assets Long-term assets that have some substance, such as buildings and equipment.

Unrestricted funds These are funds held for the general purposes of the charity, to be spent within the stated objects.

Index